And Then God Said... Th

And Then God Said...
Then *I* Said...
Then He Said...

Volume Two

Copyright © 2011 by Celest and David

This book is not a work of fiction and has been intentionally unedited.

The book cover art was designed by God and painted by Celest.

A special acknowledgement for special people.

We wish to thank Tim and Mike, our computer genius friends, and our good friend Thor for the job they have done with all the technical aspects of taking this book from its manuscript form, proofreading for typos and formatting it into book layout for the printer.

And Then God Said...
Then *I* Said...
Then He Said...

Volume Two

This book contains information God transmitted to Celestial (Celest) Blue Star of the Pleiades and David of Arcturus. In this book God continues to provide pertinent information to benefit all people regardless of their preconceived beliefs. These are the words of truth and wisdom as presented to humanity by the God of this Universe. This information is relevant to the further pursuit of truth and the debunking of the illusions that so many people on the planet still cling to.

Included in this book is a chapter that God transmitted to Chako Priest. There is also a special presentation by the Master "Kato."

God Talk

Foreword

*David...*More and more people across this glorious and unique, yes, one of a kind planet, are becoming increasingly aware that something has altered, that <u>everything</u> in fact is changing. Most of them are not aware of what is happening or why these current and other impending changes are so desperately needed. God, in His infinite wisdom has been sharing with all of us His perspectives of this monumental timeline we are all blessed to be experiencing. He ties all of this information together beautifully by showing us not only what has occurred, more importantly *what had to transpire* to get us to this tipping point in human evolution. This is the finale of the "And Then God Said..." book series and I am sure that He will be sharing with us many more of His insights about how best to proceed in the days that follow. At one point He did tell me that in order for humanity to hear most of His thoughts He would need to fill an encyclopedia just to scratch the surface. Apparently He knows this to be of importance as we are now looking forward to many more volumes in His "God Book Series."

As for me, I feel blessed, very blessed, to not only be alive at this time and to be able to bear witness first hand to the events as they unfold, but to do my part to bring clarity and wisdom to areas that lacked both. There is a momentum in motion that can not be stopped much to the chagrin of those who despise change. In the days, months and years ahead we **will** learn as a species to live together in peace and harmony. We will, as a unified race of Beings, learn to strip ourselves of our *safety nets* and *finally* begin to live as a whole **in** the moment, not **for** the moment. What grand surprises and revelations we have in store for us. Book one became affectionately known of as "The God Book" and rightly so. These are the first books where God can speak directly to us, uncensored, unedited and no one has any underlying intent to distort the speaking and sharing of Universal truths. Thus God can continue to enlighten the masses.

Celest.....Have you ever noticed that just when you think you know what you are about to do, something shifts and you find there is more that has been in the planning stages than you ever thought of? This is rather the way I felt on July 11, 2010, when God appeared and told me he wanted David and I to continue with writing a series of His books. Of course I did not question Him about this matter, what would be the point? God knows far better than anyone else does why He wants certain things to take place. Why He does what He does often remains a bit of a mystery until such time that God decides it is time to reveal the "where, how and why." On that auspicious day, after a bit more of a conversation with God about the different possibilities and probabilities He wanted to present to the people of the planet, I then went and spoke with David about this wonderful task we have been chosen to perform, "for the good of all."

God has swiftly given us the titles and the chapter names for the complete God Series. This series totals 8 books. He gave us this information before we began writing this third book. I must tell all of you with complete honesty that we can see clearly why His words are so important to every race of people on this planet. I only ask each of you to please, keep an open mind and allow your Soul Voice to override your intellect as you read these books. Also, please consider yourselves to be the chosen recipients of a great honor that God is bestowing on you. He did not <u>have</u> to extend His loving arms, His great unlimited compassion to assist anyone in overcoming their preconditioned illusions brought about by misanthropic people and energies and by their families and peers who do not know any better. If you choose to listen and understand His words, you will become a better informed person and the world will benefit by all each of you relearns. We are indeed blessed and we should all understand and appreciate this undeniable fact by taking the time to listen.

Introduction

God (*received by Celest*) Well, here **I AM** flanked by My faithful scribes once again. As Celest pointed out to all of you Children, "I have just begun." There is never too much too say, however, there is too little time to say all that needs to be said. To speak of all the issues and occurrences continuing on the planet would require more time than anyone has now.

Unfortunately.

I intentionally chose to await certain gridline intersections before I could permit any of My books to be written. So much of what I should do depended on how each Soul on this planet, including the ones who have been leaving at a steady, accelerated pace in particular over the last 20 years, behaved, believed and evolved or devolved. Children, I have told you each repeatedly, "nothing happens by chance, or happenstance or that ill-begotten term, "coincidence." I have always chosen My scribes carefully. I require so much of them and they must ALWAYS be willing to give to Me their personal best. If you think this is easy, then wait awhile. The day may come when I waggle My finger at you in a loving beckoning gesture and you will see for yourselves how difficult a task it is to not only be My scribes, but live your lives as Gods and Goddesses in activated manifestation. It means you must give up a lot, everything if necessary, and live your life without a safety harness while becoming a HUGE target for the unilluminated.

I am addressing this issue now because I have heard so many of you wondering why I chose My Celest-self and My David-self to write these books. Some have what it takes and some do not; it is all a matter of evolution and all the aspects that evolution entails. I want all of My Children everywhere to be able to relate to each of My Selves writing these books because My scribes do most aptly portray a mirror image of the majority of the *conscious* people of this planet. The "majority" in this sense means those who are now finally a part of the rapidly growing collective consciousness.

I have made a decision about the best way for you who are the Children reading this book to relate to all that I have to say. I have decided that since Celest and David are on two different levels of evolution, I will speak to David in one manner and I will speak with Celest with a different approach. So, oftentimes you will read the same information but it will be expressed by Me in a different way. It means that basically there are those of you who will understand the words of one scribe more clearly than the other. David has long been working with the initiates on this planet so he can speak with them in a way that they may be able to understand better. Celest however has been working with initiates, elders, Masters, other Star Keepers and other evolved Souls for much longer than has David. She does so in a manner that David is to some degree still becoming used to. David has been evolving at a rapid pace however and no longer has any qualms or too much humility when speaking with the Masters. I shall continue writing this way for the remainder of the God Book Series.

In this book which is the final book hosting a question and answer session, I have asked My scribes to look into the collective consciousness to glean what would be the best questions to ask Me. I have also told them to ask about any questions they themselves may have. It is in this manner that our work together can and will open many doors in the closets of your mindselves. I have chosen My topics very carefully. These are the ones I know that are the most important to address at this time. I do not ask that you all agree with Me, I do ask that you remember as you read this book that you are Me and that the more you come to terms with this truth, the better you will understand the written words. I will as usual only explain what I feel I should. I will never take away your lessons. Even though you do not **all** do your homework. Do not take it for granted that you will understand everything I say. After all, your track record is not so good, now is it? I will continue to refer to all of you as "Children or people." As far as I am concerned, there is no difference.

God (*received by David*) My Children, welcome to the first day of the rest of your natural born lives. I have awaited this moment to again speak directly with you; I have waited for these times for as long as you have been there on Earth. And rightly so, for now I can speak openly and unabashedly to each of you. Your fears, uncertainties and doubts are all about to be laid to rest by My soothing words. *Is that what you wish to hear?* Well, ok, many of you may not find comfort in knowing that you have been intentionally misled by others all these many years. However, learn you did from your mistakes, however painful these lessons may have been. At least some of you have. Nothing is "forever" in the physical realm, YOU, as Soul, however are. How can this be? Remember what I have spoken of in the past; you are eternal Souls having yet another of many physical lifetimes. Does this mean that you should not heed My words of caution to you and go back to living a life of complacency and ineptness? Of course not. You have all done that at one time or another throughout your many incarnations. Now IS the time for you to shine as your true Soul selves, as your essence demands of you.

I will proceed with this book as I did with volume 1 and answer to the best of My ability the questions that are foremost on the minds of the masses. Those of you who already know some of the answers, well, consider some of these responses as a refresher course. Creator knows... I do.

The winds of change are continually calling out to each of you, to your eternal Souls, to make the most of this lifetime. If you do your part I shall gladly do Mine and *remind* you of what many of you may have forgotten. Each tiny bell of recognition that goes off will sound with great resilience throughout the cosmos adding splendidly to the musical symphony that continually plays. I can see already that many of you are adding to this melody and that you are **now** doing so with intent. This is *music of the spheres* and I do mean that quite literally. Each tonal attunement played in the ethers contributes to the diversity which exists within the Tapestry of Life. I have spoken of this before yet it bears mentioning again. As an integral, inseparable aspect of the Creation process, each of you contributes to either the malfeasance of Spirit or the ascension of Spirit. I love that about you; to the best or worst of your abilities you are each enacting change whether you consciously know it or not. I have watched firsthand as you have assimilated My previous words to you and duly noted each of your responses. I must say they are as varied and diverse as each of you are and this IS a compliment. I would like you all to remember that My experiences are your experiences, so by all means enhance them at will.

Now as I do not wish to make My introduction too long I will simply remark that in this moment Celest and David and I are laughing and enjoying our time together. I believe they are amused by My choice of words in these, My Godumentaries. This sharing does by no means need to be limited to only these two; each of you has the ability to speak with Me directly, in fact, I would prefer it that way. Less gets lost in the translation if I speak directly to each of you on your own level and in your own *tongue.* Until such time as each of My Earthbound Children feels comfortable with reuniting with Me on this level I will pleasantly content Myself with speaking through these faithful scribes. Most of you have no idea of the amount of effort and dedication it takes to take on projects like this one of Mine. As always I am eternally grateful to all who step forward and volunteer.

God Talk 1

Basic Instructions before Entering Earth

God (*received by Celest*) Well, I would like to say that you all do indeed know how to read directions and follow instructions. I would **like** to, however that would be a blatant mistruth. Ok, I shall attempt to start at the beginning, although that was so very long ago in a realm far, far, away. That long ago era was a period of a tremendous and gracious conjunction of the complementariness of harmonics with Soul Cluster achievements combined with Soul Cluster evolutions. We were all in the higher dimensions of course, and We were blessed with the cordial visits of the Gods and Goddesses from other Universes who co-joined with Us to share in Our diverse plans for Creating new worlds and new thought patterns. There are so many dimensions and levels of dimensional understanding and dimensional harmonics and tonal patterns, Children. If you could but imagine or visualize a horizon that extends into infinity; a horizon dotted with seemingly small objects and shining lights that go on forever, just as does this horizon that I speak of, then you would at the very least have a bit of an idea of the vastness of what is called, "the realms of the knowing." It is here within these walls-less places where Soul <u>as</u> the unique ubiquitous entity It truly is, can float or travel unimpeded from one dimension to another to another, for as long as the individual Soul chooses to do so. Or, until the main OverSoul Cluster calls the Soul to return to the fold.

Here, in this place that many of you would consider to be somewhat magical, is where each Soul who is invited to visit or in some cases remain and assist other Souls, can replenish not only the individual Self, but each Soul is also deemed to be a contributing factor for the constant Creative Processing that must also be in fluid motion. Any Soul's personal thought wave can produce and enhance any and all Creative ventures. These ventures I speak of are the ones that the Universe sees to be either a possibility for the continuous uninterrupted expansion of the limitless of the realm, or a highly charged probability that right action taken and enhanced by Soul energy functioning as a collective fulcrum, can and does provide both a microcosmic and a macrocosmic view of all new life forms that can and will be Created. These Souls will either be born into or walk into life on other worlds and in other Universes for the purpose of asexual propagation of new, more highly refined life species. OK, so it is when these Souls' personal thought waves are focused on any issue, venture, or even their personal conceptualization of what can or may cause a better wave of new thoughts and better life patterns, that new worlds, those not Created in their entirety yet, exist in a type of miniature "holding area." It is here that they are each awaiting all the matter required to build a sphere comprised of the best of the best of all energetic matter. This energetic matter is in a direct correlation with all conditions needing to be met to build a better place in a better time. This is all a part of what I consider to be, "Spatial Understanding." This may be difficult for some people to empathize with while Earthbound, but when the Souls in these realms are focusing on a certain issue or schematic undertaking, they each also have the innate ability to have their mind thoughts meander in a focused manner into many different areas *all at the same time.* Essentially this means that they are in point A, B, C and so on simultaneously. Think of it as an example of being a "real know it all." When not Earthbound, Souls simply have the ability they were Created with; they are able to know, be, see, formulate and understand all things at the same time...unless they choose not to. That however, does not happen very often.

Some people here on the Earth Star refer to "dimensional thoughts" yet do not know what it really means. It is in fact a Creative venture by which all things for the betterment of each Universe can be Created by the sheer magnitude of the thought-wave itself being propelled by the motivation, Soul desire and determination to succeed for the good of each Universe, that lies in the form of the Individual Soul and group Soul Cluster. The Creator is always seeking more new worlds with more advanced life forms to set into motion as part of the eternal Creative processing. This of course requires the slow but steady forward progression of mind, body and Spirit of each life species on each world in each Universe. It is here where Souls co-join, especially after leaving the tyrannical mind projections that so many of My Earthbound Children still adhere to on this planet. These returning Souls then begin to seek better ways to arm themselves Spiritually if they do indeed need to return to the planet for reasons of either personal destiny or planetary destinations. Obviously, after any period of time spent on Earth, Souls require some extensive and intensive rest and aid from their Guides and Master Teachers. Some more than others.

The Gods and Goddesses from all Universes, whom Celest has named as a collective, *"The Luminescents,"* rely in a sense on the ideas, actions and Creative abilities of all the Souls who gather together in the realms of the knowing. While here, many, many, many, Star Keeper Children from other planets also in this realm do also add their own accumulated knowing and wisdom to the inventiveness of the Creation processing. This processing is quite capable of formulating on its own many new trends and physical attributes needed to have all new life species be better able to comport themselves through the process of adaptation to new physical surroundings on new worlds. However it is when the great gathering of the Souls take place and each One contributes to the mass thoughts and recognizes the need for all new worlds to be able to be self-sustaining and truly "democratic" in the manner of Creating and believing in true freedom in life, that the pieces of the Universal puzzle easily fall into place as each Soul, each visiting entity, each of the Luminescents, contribute to the WHOLE. **This** Children, is how life is originally Created.

You see, I am not speaking in any terms that are definitions of what you have termed, "linear." Linear is but an illusion, albeit it had been a necessary one for Earth for too long. The Creation and propagation of life is a spatial understanding of gridline intersections and Creative **conceptions** brought together in a homogeneous fashion. You have each begun as the most minute speck of Light imaginable. In our own non-time honored traditions, each new speck of this incandescent matter blasts into manifestation as a new genesis of thought and thought projections. You each whirl and sway your essence into small groups while each Soul adds more luster and glow to the co-aligned energy matter. You are BORN **as** Soul yet you are born **from** Soul. OK, now here is where it may be difficult to explain this second part in a simple fashion. Each Soul carries a TYPE of gene; a TYPE of molecular interplay that carries within its own matrix, Creative thought forms and images from other worlds.

However, what My Earth scientists still do not want to understand is that as this "phenomena" occurs, you each ALSO bear the special gene that is part of the Creator's own life force as well as the genes from whatever planet you will have chosen as your "home base." Essentially this means that whoever the Luminescent is who is the governing Care Taker of any Universe, also shares with you a symbiotic and sympathetic unbreakable cord sometimes known as *"the silver umbilical cord."* As for MySelf, yes, I have shared my inner SELF with each of you who arrives here. At one point or another. When a Soul departs the mortal life and returns to Nirvana that Soul still retains My indelible fingerprint as well as the ones from the other Luminescents whom that Soul has spent time with. Every time a Soul spends "time" on another world, this obviously includes the worlds in My own Universe as well, those Souls unconsciously adapt and integrate with the vibrations and frequencies that are the dominant ones on that world. **If** those vibrations and frequencies are deemed to be too harsh, too unmelodious or too lower based for those Souls, they have the God-given right to alter those energies by seeking out and aligning with the ones that do in fact correspond with whatever part or parts of the individual Soul that is untarnished. This is a major reason why so many of you here have never been able to find contentment with those of "lesser minds." Although it is true that all Souls receive instructions prior to their launching into a life other than the higher dimensional life, I am only dealing with the Earth Star planet in this chapter.

Souls mature quickly, <u>in one sense,</u> after they have transformed from the tiny particle of non-carbon based energy into a Light that usually appears to be twinkling. Because this process is a constant continuation of growth that occurs from moment-to-moment, it is necessary to have all the Spirit Guides, designated Master Teachers and Star Keeper representatives from each world to be present to assist the new Lights during their quest for understanding. Just like all Children should, all new Souls delight in expressing their individual appreciation and limitless joy while discovering more and more other "family" members to converse with. There is nothing here that would in any manner be confused with, "a mind is a terrible thing to waste." That simply would not do. I must say it is intriguing to listen to all the telepathy that is ongoing during these early and vitally important stages.

Before the system of distinguishing events between how much a Soul should know on their maiden voyage and when the appropriate gridline intersection has arrived for that departure, all probable and possible scenarios are presented to the Soul who will make the journey. No, no one will say, "watch out for that bad intersection on highway 612 on January 12, 2012." We deal in absolutes, positives and negatives when cautioning all soon-to-be departing Souls. We also teach of the power of thoughts and the power of transgressions and the road that curves that sometimes barely separates the two. Each Soul may choose their missions unless of course I have already formulated My plans for certain Souls. When the Souls arriving here will be "first timers," that life experience will be a type of catapult or conversely, a type of roadblock that will impact on future journeys here. It is all a matter of Soul choice. The greatest lessons each Soul receives from Us as a collective, are the ones that are centered on how to behave and believe and consciously expand awareness when surrounded by the hordes of humans who do none of this.

All these incoming Souls carry with them a type of silent alarm; one that sounds at *predestined* times that are determined by their mentors as the ones when their charges will most likely need succor and encouragement. These determinations are made predicated by the teachers' abilities to focus, or fast-forward, into the future to see how well their charges have listened and learned. Even then of course all possible venues, all probable meetings with others of the Soul Clusters is also taken into account. Souls do of course have the free expression to simply say, "No, I do not like this place after all. Can I go home now?" At that point unless the remark is simply either facetious or a means of venting in order to release mental or emotional pressure, the wisdom of the Sages is presented to them in tiny doses. For some of My Children this method works most admirably. They simply pick themselves up and start over again. For others...their wish is their command.

You see, the id factor is always in a prominent place- one that encompasses heart, Soul and mind desire. All actions predicated upon "right actions to take" then transfer into a small section of the id where that initial placement CAN or MAY gain in prominence. This of course affects all aspects of the individual's personality as well as acting as a type of "tuning fork." The Earth Star walk can be fraught with great difficulties; I acknowledge this fact completely. However, you never leave home without possessing all the necessary instructions to guide you each on your journey. This is true of all lifetimes, not merely the present one you are living. Unfortunately, well, it seems to be unfortunate to many Earthbound Souls; they want to have all the routes in life spelled out for them in totality. Then of course their walk would be a breeze. They would have nothing to do; nothing to learn or relearn. Some would actually welcome this. HOWEVER, I will **NEVER** permit that! I see that My Celestial-self is chomping at the bit to present some questions, so We shall move on for that.

Celest...God, when you speak of so many dimensions and dimensional understandings, would you please explain to readers some of these levels? Perhaps it would help them to better understand these particular events and realities that may not have been adequately explained to them before.

God...All right, I agree that could be a great help to the Children. Dimensions exist on many, many, levels of density and non-density. Some are pure vibrations that encompass a certain configured and calibrated degree (*ranges) of a **type** of thought housed within a citadel of a concentric and concentrated mass of energy that is an extension of the Creative processing UNIT. This particular unit is either a small mass or a huge mass depending on the accumulative vibrations of the pure energy. A small mass may become greater than it had been in its initial stages, just as a huge mass may become smaller as more energy leaves the matrix of that area in order for the departing energy to move forward into a more elevated or evolved state of itself. "Density" in this sense simply denotes the degree and angle of a concentrated mass. It is not in any manner less important than the units composed of non-density. Each unit exists with many levels, many stages, of non-matter resting in a sense within each level as part of the necessary growth patterns. This is also true of the units of non-density. Energy CAN at times be a heavy mass. <u>At times</u>. The age, components and previous conditions of the energies for example, define which type of unit those energies of non-matter shall inhabit for a specified period of time. "Time" in this sense is merely a unit of measurement not to be equated with anything linear.

It is when a certain type of transformation has taken place that a dark, perhaps cloudy looking mass, can alter into a lighter more refined image of itself. When this occurs it means that these types of denser energies may leave and journey on to other worlds or assist in Creating world events. Those masses inhabiting the non-density areas can also redefine themselves and become translucent if that is what their energies require in order for them to inhabit other worlds in other dimensions. Then of course there are the dimensions that exist far above the Earth Star planet where "thought and Soul" rule those dimensions. These are the areas that are <u>for the most part</u> housing ancient civilizations, many that you have never even heard of. Other dimensions house other worlds, other Universes, where yet again thought and Soul are the prominent de facto life force energies housing many, many, life forms you have no memory of. All of these types of dimensions exist in "realms." These realms are....more refined, more evolved life-support star systems than this planet Earth is. These dimensions in **these** types of realms can and must only be entered by certain types of Beings. Furthermore, they can only be inhabited by the evolved Children of all worlds. Even though in fact, many of these dimensions house only animal, flora and fauna life forms. Of course all of My Star Keeper Children from other planets also exist in their own dimensions, (realms.)

Essentially the dimensional realms are citadels; each one is a type of specialist. Each one possesses its own characteristics, its own area of "expertise." I spoke of the Crystal City in volume 1. That citadel too exists in its own dimension. Other realms have certain specialties as well. One dimension may be an "event" that hosts all the most learned scientific minds in **that particular Universe.** Another realm may host all the most beneficial and advanced form of hydroponic foods. Although as I have stated all realms have their missions, their appointed tasks to fulfill, it is important that you each understand that they do work in tandem in order that their own individualized roles function "*in toto.*" I do not expect all of you to completely understand My explanations here, however the most simple way is to merely say they flow in synchronized fashion.

Celest...God, please explain further about dimensional realms' specialties and dimensional thinking and how it is part of the basic instructions.

God...Ok, I will add to My previous statements; there is a realm that incorporates the "knowing" accrued by each Soul on an individual basis that can and does easily ascertain how much that particular Soul would need in order to return to this planet and be more enabled to once again fight the good fight. I am of course referring to the resumption of overcoming Earthbound challenges in order to relocate the motivation and Soul desire to evolve. Here in this realm I am speaking of, is where infinite information is available on the "single Soul" basis and is filtered into the matrix of that individual Soul. As this occurs this information is also filtered into the Greater Consciousness of that Soul's own Soul Cluster. This in turn allows the main OverSoul Cluster to also receive this information. In this manner not only the Soul Cluster that this Soul belongs to is receiving this data, it also enables the main OverSoul Cluster to readily identify all weaknesses and strengths that have either been overcome by the Soul, or conversely, what weaknesses and strengths are **at that present moment** afflicting that Soul. This is part of the evolutionary process. This is just one manner that the individual Soul Cluster and the main OverSoul can assist in the Creation of life forms who have greater abilities, thus causing them to be less prone to believing misconceptions about true realities.

Again this is but one realm that I am speaking of. It simply is not possible to speak of them all. Their numbers are too vast. "Dimensional thinking" is merely a term used to denote how the "knowing" that resides within each Soul can and does enable the Creative processing to better ascertain what degree of learning should be incorporated within the psyche of each soon-to-be reincarnating Soul. As each Soul moves forward in gathering more understanding about ItSelf, that data integrates with many, many, others who are part of the incoming Souls' groups and are also part of the "knowing" that is dormant for the most part, that each one who is of EACH Soul Cluster will now possess. So it is that if person "A" arrives on one part of the planet and person "B" arrives on the other side of this world yet each possesses a unified field of knowing SHARED by them both, even though in all likelihood they will never meet one another in the physical, they share a telepathic communication that in most cases they are not aware of. The level of consciousness they share will be of an equal level, one with the other. Even though it may be unconscious, it still does exist and is of paramount importance to their chosen life experiences. Now multiply those two Souls by millions of incoming Souls who also share the same thought patterns and dimensional thinking. "Thought" is merely an energetic movement of the psyche and the Soul ItSelf. It is indeed a force to be reckoned with.

I will speak briefly of one other realm, however. I do so because of the vital role it plays in the synchronized movement of Soul Cluster energies that merit and display the beauteous and tangibly intangible glory of the Tapestry of Life. The realm of *the dream world* interplays and interacts with ALL the designated missions and responsibilities of all reincarnating Souls. As part of the processing of the basic instructions you each possess, you also have the great benefits you receive through dreams and visions that are interpreted by the Soul in a far different manner than your intellect interprets them. All dimensional thoughts, especially those being sent to you by members of your Soul Cluster, pass through the dream realm just as you all agreed to. Of course each Guide and Master Teacher also has the privilege of speaking with you and to you, and sometimes through you per your Soul Contract. This Soul agreement must be adhered to by all Souls everywhere, particularly on Earth. Those who choose not to support this Contract will have serious consequences to contend with.

The dream realm contains multitudinous information that is correlated for your remembering what you should remember and simultaneously allowing certain information to remain dormant in the part of your mind that Celest and David refer to as, "your hard drive." You see, all this is relevant to you in order for each of you to at the very least develop a CONSCIOUS understanding that you do indeed know more than you are aware of. Even a modicum of understanding is worth ten times more than an illusion. By the way, I will only tell you one bit of information you received before you descended to this planet. One of the basic instructions given to all of My Children is, *"to err is human...just don't do it too much."*

David....You stated that some realms specialize in hydroponic foods. Can you briefly explain to us the reasoning behind the diversity of life here on this planet and why it was chosen to be this way?

God*....*David, this IS My world. As I expressly spoke of above, each new world, each new civilization that is Created is done so with the utmost care and diligence. In this manner no two are ever the same nor should they be. Earth was to be a playground of sorts, *after* she ceased to be a schoolhouse planet. She was always intended to be a destination of respite for the weary, as well as adventurous enough for the intrepid explorer. There are many worlds now that have such diversity; at the time of Terra's Creation there were not nearly as many as there are now. The Creator, the Creation and the Creative Process as well as MySelf desired to Create a planet that would stimulate the thoughts, minds and hearts and procreate further Creativity of the science-minded as well as the dreamer and poet amongst you. Turn left, turn right, whichever way you choose to turn, this world offers diversity and limitless bounty; true oodles of abundance, which sadly most of you ignore. Vacationers on Earth deem it necessary to travel long distances simply to explore something new, yet sadly most have never walked more than twenty steps from their own front yard to see what it is I have Created for them just across the way.

As for the civilizations that specialize in hydroponic food production, yes, this is most certainly true. If you had conscious recall of all your past lives and were able to access the memories of the many lifetimes when you incarnated on other worlds you *would* recall many fond memories of working in the hydroponic field. There are many worlds that dedicate themselves to the service of others by growing foods to support themselves as well as cultures from other worlds. As the human body continues to evolve, *transform itself*, you will find that the body will no longer need to support itself from the nutrients found only in the meat provided by the animal kingdom. Also most of what is typically termed junk food will no longer exist simply because the body will not crave it any longer. The same will be true with pharmaceuticals, once the body adapts to the new frequencies all disease will be eradicated and artificial drugs will thankfully fade from recognition into bad memories of the past which need not be repeated. For now the human vehicle still needs to sustain itself with the nutrients that are readily available on this world. So give your body what it needs. The time for you to alter your eating habits and become strict vegetarians is not yet at hand. This transition will come naturally, be patient. **Do not try to force evolution.** Remember, remember, the Universe is always on time. How's that?

David....Excellent. Thank you.

God (*received by David*) Ok, let us move on to part two of this writing with no further ado. David's mind is dashing too and fro wondering what it is that I might deem of importance to tell you here. Now mind you he has no idea what I am speaking to Celest about while she types her part on the computer next to him. I prefer it that way, there are no influences that may contribute to duplicating information between the two, or I should say, the three of Us.

My Children, let us talk bluntly here for time is short for many people. I would like to share with you a bit of information about what you agreed to before incarnating there on Earth. Each of you knew beforehand that it would not always be an easy task you undertook. Living life with a "physical body" and *preferably* venturing forth without wearing a life preserver while living life without any *remembrances* of who you really were and what your chosen roles and lessons would be in any given lifetime, did not deter you in the slightest from your desire to test yourself mightily and to succeed. And test yourselves you did. We have spoken in the past about Soul Contracts so I will not go into that in this message. Suffice it to say that all of you wrote your own contracts, dotted each "I", crossed each "T" and went over your lesson plans with all the others in your Soul Clusters, as well as other Soul Clusters, who you would directly or indirectly interact with in each lifetime. Yes, nearly ALL of you have incarnated here on

Earth time and time again. Initially each of you went boldly forth into your first incarnation knowing, but not necessarily *in totality* understanding, what life would be like for you in a physical world and the demands that could be put on you for your basic survival. How could you? Living the experience is far different from watching the movie or reading about it. Let's face it, the density this world's populace descended into by the actions and influences of those less stouthearted Souls made each of your Earth Star walks much more difficult than they were ever intended to be. Back in the earliest beginnings of the human race you were informed that it would indeed require many incarnations before the human race would be deemed ready to ascend to a higher level of consciousness. Move forward to the present now and I will enlighten those who are the still doubtful. Yes, you did know exactly what you were getting into. How do I describe the denseness of this world compared to how it might have been? The denseness has been like swimming in molasses. If life had progressed as was possible, instead of a hostile environment of quicksand mixed with molasses, you would be enjoying an intimate relationship with each other as well as with the planet herself. I did not choose this for you; the decision has always been made by the masses in the Universally honored tradition of allowing free expression to be your guide. Yes, you had some outside influences beckoning to unsettle you, yet it was and in many ways still is, the group mentality that governs change. If you want to know what this world *could have been* like, I invite you to revisit her in a couple hundred of your Earth years.

For many of you, you bit off more than you could chew by trying to accomplish too much in any one time. Far be it from Me to stand in your way. However, you see it is far different to decide you wish to accomplish this and that and then find out that without your ***water wings*** you could not swim in the deep end of the pool. Now I am not saying this to in any way demean you or discourage you, this is simply an observation. Very few people can soar with the eagles until they have first fluttered about a bit. Fortunately for you there are always contingency plans that are enacted in your behalf in case something does not go according to your desires. In other words, there is always a Plan B and a Plan C to fall back upon as I have told you before. This is why it was always intended for each of you to have multiple incarnations to try and get it right, whatever **it** was you were intending to accomplish. Well... more so to **your** personal satisfaction. No, there is no right and wrong, just varied degrees of ways and means to accomplish a goal.

Before anyone begins to falter here, let Me clarify something that is still prevalent in many of your minds. There are no sins, only errors in judgment. There are no sin-eaters either, as I have told you previously. Nor can another purge you of your preconceived sins by confessing them, I spoke of this before as well. I do not judge you, you do a pretty good job of that all by yourself. Furthermore you do a self-examination when you experience your *past life review* which occurs after you transition from the physical realm. You may relate it to a time when you first learned to begin the self-examination process as you grew and matured. The strictest critic of oneself is Self. Others may be judgmental, however you are in charge of your own destinies and the decisions you made along the way. This is not to say that there are not outside influences which may challenge you every chance they get. These moments are a test of your endurance and dedication to Self to stay the course.

Because this is My book, I shall from time to time remind you of tidbits of wisdom that I shared with you previously.

Now back to what you knew, or what you **believed** you knew. Incarnating is a growth process which most, not all, Souls go through. Each chooses which planet they wish to incarnate on, what their expectations of that lifetime are and whether they shall incarnate in a masculine or feminine form. Each carries its own learning curve. Ok, yes, for those who still don't know or perhaps some of you still do not want to accept it, your roles in each lifetime have been as diverse as the stars overhead in the night sky. Isn't life grand? If you don't like who you are, next time change the role you will be playing. That having been said.. if you do not like yourself in this lifetime, then by all means change yourself in the present. Only you can do that. You have always had the power, yet few have exercised their God-given rights to use it to its full potential. As I said, the Earth Star walk is not easy for anyone, so lose any thoughts that others have it so much easier than you do, for they do not. They each have their own trials and tribulations to deal with. Let us move on now shall we?

Now since you know you have Soul Contracts and you know that you can change who you are at any given time let us examine some of the more basic of the basics. Each one of you has the option to alter your own destiny at any given moment; evidence of this is abundant all around you. I ask that you look at all those Souls who are choosing of their own free expression (free will) to leave this world when the going gets tough. You can and do choose to enter into an agreement with another Soul for a specific purpose before incarnating and then during the incarnation you have the option to alter that agreement. This happens more often than most would imagine. There are many reasons for this, although I won't go into in detail about that at this moment. Suffice it to say that *you changed your mind.* This is allowed. The overall goal here is to contribute to the ascension of not only your Spirit but to contribute to that of others as well. You do this by teaching by example. If you still do not know what I mean, perhaps it is time for you to take a refresher course in "Understanding Life 101."

Each Soul that transcends from the higher realms to undertake a life with a body and emotions and all else that goes along with having a physical vehicle, understands that at some point they may become ensnared by the irrational, unpredictable and sometimes unscrupulous behavior that is prevalent when a species severs its connection with the Divine. In this sense, I refer to The Divine as "Myself." You all have witnessed this firsthand at one time or another. Again, this is what happens when a newborn Soul is somehow, at some time, for whatever reason coerced into believing they must grow up and follow another's beliefs. Although this act is unintentional for the <u>most</u> part on the part of the teacher. I encourage all of you to mature, to evolve, however I never once said you have to grow up and act like adults. Be astonished, thrilled and absolutely enchanted by all that your senses present you with. Far too many "Adults" are irrational for they only process information on second or third dimensional levels. This simply will not do if one is to rise above the limited confines of a primitive or immature society. You must take personal responsibility for your choices or others **will** make your decisions for you. You never, ever, have to assume any liability for the choices of OTHERS. Do you understand? I have stated this before, however this is still too prevalent on this planet. Knowing and understanding this should lessen or at the very least reveal the tethers that try to bind you to the lower vibrations. And yes, by all means, it IS all right to be disappointed in others, remember?

Another basic that is taught to each Soul is that at one point or another you may be targeted by the lesser evolved ones around you. Proximity plays a keen role in this. You must know how and when to protect yourself from these onslaughts. The simplest and easiest way to do this is to **know when to leave.** If that does not work then I suggest you rise merrily up into your happiest, most jubilant self. In this exalted state of being, you are emitting a light source that is virtually impenetrable. Your aura, your body's natural electrical field, will repel/displace any lower type of denseness that has permeated your personal aura. If you don't believe Me then try it. You are in no way limited to doing this when only in close proximity. Project your unfettered thoughts of love and gratitude out into the world with Spiritual intent and see what happens. This is a simple method of cleansing and dispelling negative thoughts and emotions. I would be amiss if I did not tell you at this juncture that not all lesser evolved beings respond well to random acts of kindness. To them, love and happiness mix together as well as oil and water. So be prepared to ask for help when needed, I do not expect you to do it all by yourself.

Let us speak about the rewards you receive from both positive and negative experiences for a moment. Each of you knows how to treat yourself to something special. Do you also know that when you treat yourself to something that is not always pleasant or satisfying you also receive a reward? *Wisdom comes from knowledge and knowledge cannot be acquired without first having the experience.* Think on that for a moment. Life throws you curveballs from time to time just to see if you are paying attention. It also does this to make sure you have learned your lesson and remember please, life is always about lessons. Sometimes the most rewarding experience can be the one that you never, ever wish to repeat. Many of you seem to have these experiences yet refuse to break free from the circumstances that created them in the first place. Take for example those that have become co-dependent upon others.

Whether in the first tense or the second tense, it matters naught. Each is dependent upon another to fill a void that has remained empty by not taking care of <u>number one</u> first. You have heard Me say from time to time that you must be your own best friend first before you can be another's. The same applies to loving another or *accepting* the love of another. If you are co-dependent upon another's approval of yourself then how are you ever going to move forward? If you force your dependency on another are you really doing them any favors? I think not. You all know someone who bailed another person out of a situation that they got themselves into. Some of these *paroled* people learn right away not to repeat the situation. Others continue to do the same thing over and over again expecting a different result each time.

Let Me paraphrase some of this for you. Life on many worlds is not always the same as being on your home worlds where honesty, trust, compassion, an innate understanding of right and wrong and giving freely of unfettered amounts of unconditional love and sharing are the most basic of instincts. Let's face it, the people of this world can be cruel and ugly, remember that this is not an illusion, an attitude or a projection that can be altered simply because you deem it necessary to be done. Replenishing one's mind, body and Spirit is essential to your survival. If you don't know how, then it IS time to learn. And please, don't expect changes to happen overnight. It has taken many a millennia to get mass consciousness to its current state of awareness; it will take a while longer for it to rise to its next level. This will require the combined effort of all people everywhere to desire change for the better. This does not mean you should join the delusional; if they ask you for help then offer them a better alternative to the reality they are currently living. Having a life worth living is your birthright yet it is up to you to bring it into manifestation. I can lead you to a Spiritual oasis, yet it is up to you whether to replenish yourselves in it or not. And yes, this too is important, YOU were informed you may lose your connectedness with All That Is, it is up to you to first recognize this when it does happen and second, to do something about it. You all know what to do; it is up to you to do it. Always try to see the positive rather than the negative. Try to see the good in everyone, but for NIRVANA's sake don't allow yourself to be pulled into another's dark reality, especially when that reality does not align with your own. There are enough dramas being played out in this world; separate yourself from them if you intend to survive the coming days. Others will try to subtly coerce you to their way of thinking with flattery and false visions of hope and grandeur. Remember that I gifted each of you with a brain.... Use it.

You have, I have, We have, provided everything you require to fulfill your personal as well as planetary destinies. Never doubt that. Never doubt yourself or you will be setting yourself up to fail. Remember that the mind plays tricks on people from time to time. Learn to discern when something is right for you. Once again I ask you to listen to your Soul Voice, It will never steer you wrong. Your intellect was trained by you, to service you, to bow to your every whim and desire as well as to protect you from your own insecurities. Its main purpose is to protect you... not always from yourself. Your Soul cannot be influenced so easily. Learn to meld the two, bring them into harmony with one another, all that is required for this to happen is for you to get out of your own way.

Education is the key element in formatting a concise lifetime of stimulating, awe-inspiring experiences. So We educated you, now it is time you to further educate yourself by looking into your past experiences and learning from these. Life, regardless of where you are geographically or Spiritually, is diverse and subject to change. You learn to adapt, you learn to improvise; you depart from the path of least resistance to learn new things. This world like none other is not for the faint of heart. It is for the bold, the unwavering, the upwardly mobile. If this appeals to you then you ARE in the right place at the right time. If it does not then perhaps you were not as prepared for this lifetime as you thought. As the populations of this world dwindle down to a mere fraction of what they had been, those left standing will have gone the distance and freed themselves from any encumbrances that may have previously held them at bay. The ones that may have kept them from being their true God Self. Yes, I am speaking of God I AM. This world like any other world benefits greatly when aligned with My Song.

We will not go into more detail with David at this time for as any good teacher knows, the student must come to their own conclusions on what comes next. The student must learn to read between the lines and locate the underlying truths. I am sure all of you are up to this challenge. If you have made it this far into My books then you do have the desire to know. Now it is up to you to apply what you have learned, separate what resonates with you with what does not and toss the latter aside. Mold yourself; shape yourself into the unique being that you are. It is not difficult. I remind you again, you made it this far did you not? The Universe awaits you.

David....I am curious, why choose now to introduce information about this subject? Is this not something that should have already been known about?

God....No, David, no one is allowed to come in knowing everything, you know this. If everyone knew in advance of their pre-birth agreements or the instructions they had departed with, their Spiritual and physical lives would be altered. I ask you, if you had known ahead of time about what you would be doing now, would that have not set you up with preconceived notions of what was to be? No, you do not need to answer that, I will listen to your and others' responses as they reach the end of this book. Next question please.

David....Are the instructions given differently for those who are born-in as well as those who are walk-ins?

God....Of course.

David....Do the basic instructions alter for different timelines, if so were we all encouraged to be exceptionally well prepared for this one?

God....Although most timelines in the course of Earth's history have been turbulent; this particular one is troubling for most people who choose not to recognize its importance. Try for a moment to imagine an equation, one in which the variables alter at every given moment. This is the Universe in constant motion. Insert yourself into the equation with variables unknown and try to determine the outcome of any scenario. Due to the rapid alterations as well as altercations about possibilities and probabilities the answer will never be an absolute. In this sense nothing is absolute. I mention this because far too many still believe in untrue prophesies, predictions and resolute outcomes. If this were true this Universe as well as all others would cease to be. Change is the only Constant, embrace it and flourish would be My recommendation.

David....If we all received the "same memo" why is it that the inhabitants of Earth still cannot seem to simply "get along?"

God....They will, in time. Most still cannot and will not see themselves in others. More still cannot fathom their integration with all other forms of life. And furthermore, still many others want to skate through life without any bumps in the road. Until everyone can treat a stone or a handful of dirt with the respect and admiration they too deserve, life will not alter because egos, fears and one-up-edness will prevail and unsubstantiated insecurities will not subside. Thankfully the will and determination of this planet herself will continue to change this for you.

David....I just heard someone prompt me with the words "crafty dodgers," what is that about?

God....you all know them, they are the ones that erroneously believe they are pulling the wool over others' eyes and feel, when not directly confronted, that they will *eternally* get away with it. They believe if they are careful enough, cunning enough, and keep their thoughts to themselves they can say or think one thing while silently, in an unscrupulous fashion, think or do something else. They believe no one else knows. The collective "We" know, Soul knows for sure and others eventually will as well. This is common knowledge in the Continuum. Have no qualms about who you are, be yourself and acknowledge you are that way **by choice.** Enough said.

God Talk 2

Time as a Placebo

God (*received by Celest*) Although there are many Greater Realities that can and do function as "antidotes," the linear concept of "time," has been vastly misunderstood, although I know for a fact that both Celest and her father Blue Star have both written extensively on this subject. Love can be considered as both an antidote to curb hate as well as the wondrous energetic mass that it truly is. Obviously I consider love to be the perfect cure-all and not just because I MySelf AM love. However, time and the conceptual understanding of time are as far from fact as anything can be. Unlike love. In the beginnings that predate the earliest of planetary "times" here, humankind was more intent on the barest ability to survive and paid very close, very scrupulous attention to the rising and setting of the sun and the moon and so forth. While My Star Keeper Children from other planets were here working with the earliest people, the Star Keepers formulated a plan that they felt was necessary in order to cause the early human races to learn to live together in a more harmonious fashion. At least that was the plan. It was to also incorporate the teaching to the people of the necessity of learning when to allow the physical vehicles the necessary allotments of day and night phases for replenishment of the body, mind and Spirit. This had to be accomplished slowly of course, in order for the people to educate themselves and be able to live on this planet in a healthy manner.

Many problems ensued however because the early Children usually preferred to hunt animals at night for that was when most animals come out. Also there was the disturbing habit the Children had of hunting one another at night as well. It was during these earlier times that animals themselves changed; many became meat eaters and the predator and prey forces were born. Twas not the way I intended this to be at all. However, having a governing agent, "time," Created seemed to be the most efficient method of beginning to teach the people about things to do and when to do them. If nothing else it did give them some constructive things to do. Well, some of them anyway.

My Star Keeper Children taught the people about planting crops, raising herbs and other edible plants. They learned about making fire and controlling it as well. Some of them learned, that is. As the allotments of day and night phases continued people learned to study the Sun and plan their movements around that Orb. Cloudy days did also confuse that issue however and eclipses were just not understood at all! Unfortunately as the epochs of days and years continued time was believed to be the controlling factor in everyone's lives. Sun dials evolved into watches, calendars, clocks and so forth. And what a mess humankind has made out of calendars! My Earthbound Children have become obsessed with time. As ludicrous as it is, I must ask how anyone can become so frantic over something that does not exist? Time is nothing more than a linear experience. It is not an event; it is an application of an experience. In some cases this linear experience has prevented some instances of mayhem and murder. In the worst instances however, the physical body still does not receive the type of rest and relaxation it truly needs and in other cases, people simply procrastinate their lives away.

Believing in the linear can and does also promote laziness, procrastination and living lives without any designated purpose. Soul Voice can not respond well to the personality when the personality has been captured by "time." Voice at that point becomes so muffled virtually no one will be able to hear, let alone respond. Unfortunately, My unilluminated Children lost little time in seeing how continually reinforcing linear time would work to their advantage. They did do as a means of building a stop-gate, a mind-block, that would effectively keep My other Children from **remembering** to live in the NOW. Many

Children of today use this linear time experience as an excuse for not starting projects, for not finishing projects and worst of all, for not doing anything more than they think they have to. "Time" is the great placatory agent. It epitomizes redundancy. No, none of Us could remove the beliefs you each had about the genuine existence of time. That would be intervention. You should all know by **now** how We feel about that!

I simply had to await the gridline intersection when the "knowing" of this illusion would be revealed to you, either by your own Soul or by others who do know better than do you. To further complicate this matter, although We would have dearly loved to simply eradicate the conditioning you each succumbed to, organized religions had their stake in defining time as well. TOO WELL. They invented a time of birth and death that they claimed one of My Sons, Jesus THE Christ, had been birthed and died. Of course this is untrue, BUT people clamored to believe in what is simply the unbelievable. The Illuminati Children chortled about their victory in continuing to deceive the masses. I am including this fact because I hear faint stirrings in some readers' minds about WHY We did not put a stop to that lie too. We can only do what We can only do. All right now, before I permit Celest to ask her questions, I will add just a bit more. The NOW is a simultaneous event. I have stated this before but from what I have seen this FACT is falling on deaf ears. That simply will not do! You have difficulty in understanding the NOW because you never heard about it until I and a few others attempted to explain this to all who would listen. All right Celest, I am ready.

Celest...God, I know you realize that to explain things to people who do not really want to know, can be a gesture in futility. I also know that you realize the dangers to the physical vehicle caused by people who work swing shifts and the abominable 11pm to 7am shifts. Yet until such non-time that humans realize they have capitulated and lost themselves to illusionary matter, how can You or we expect them to truly desire to understand the NOW?

God...Easy now Celest, I can feel your intense frustration about this matter. How many times have I advised you dear Child, to be content in accepting the fact that you can only teach those who ask you for help? How many times as I watched you and listened to your own thoughts have you been so frustrated and distressed by the fact that so many otherwise good people will lose their lives simply because they are too afraid to believe the REAL truth? Each time Celestial, I counseled you by reminding you that although you know all this intellectually, your Soul desire to help others sometimes overwhelms you.

When this occurs I have heard you wonder if you are doing any good here at all.

Celest, the illusion of time is something you know all about. I ask you here and NOW to remember that it is only the Children who are willing to stop believing in the faulty and misdirected beliefs of others who will be the ones to survive the continuing changes and then must bear witness themselves to the non-existence of "time." I do know the difficulty My words about the NOW present to the Children who simply do not know any better. All right, Celest, although I have spoken about this in My last book, *"Beyond the Veil, Epiphanies from God,"* I will attempt this time around to offer the most simple explanation I can and I will be brief. If the Children do not get it now, by the time they do understand it will be too late for them.

Children, you are watching a video in your home that offers a split screen movie. So, as you watch one side of the screen you can see what is happening in one place, yet at the same time but in a **different** place on the other side of the TV screen, you are watching what is occurring there as well. So essentially you are viewing 2, possibly more, events all taking place simultaneously, yet the locales are thousands of miles apart. OK, that is a miniature version of the NOW. It is a simultaneously integrated event comprised of both past, present and probable or possible futures. Yet it is all occurring at the same nano-moment. This is in great part because your pasts determine the possibilities of your presents which determine the probabilities of your futures. Do you see? There is only one governing agent in the NOW; that agent is the combination of your own mind, your intent, your Spiritual level of evolvement and your SELF-CREATED personal destiny.

In other words Children, the NOW always existed, long before any of you did, the NOW was there. Whether or not you flow with this realm or choose to remain in ignorance of it, will determine your possible and probable future placement on another orb, in another realm, in a definitive future lifetime.

Celest...God, thank you for that explanation; perhaps this will help the people to understand it better. It is very simple to understand it from my own perspective, but I do readily agree that just because I know about it and understand it, that does not mean everyone else will. Besides God, I have serious *placebo issues.* I absolutely will have nothing to do with placebos!

God...Yes, Celest I know ALL about those little issues you spoke of. You just would not be you if you were any other way. Now, I shall move on to our David.

God (*received by David*) Ok, now that Celest's unwavering, justifiable, semi-pent-up frustration is expelled for the moment let us proceed. This chapter will be shorter than the rest simply because there is only so much I can teach you about the topic at hand. Generally someone either grasps a concept or they don't. Since time is an illusion, what about the words that some of you relate to its existence. Take for example one of My favorites, "there are only ten shopping days left before Christmas." Oh, by the way, My Son Jesus, loves that one. Does this mean that His birthday will never come about again? "What happens if I do not take advantage of this *once in a lifetime shopping* opportunity, will the world cease to be?" Let's be realistic here; no single occasion, surely not one as commercialized as this one will lead to the end of a civilization. This world will keep on spinning, the Sun will keep on rising and the stock market, well, it will do what it does best, for a "time" that is. It will keep on creating illusionary fortunes for those who still require the stability of this archaic institution to bring meaning and purpose to their lives. My gosh Children, how many different ways do I need to express to you that if you take everything you have come to rely on as an absolute and whisk it away in one brief moment, humanity as a whole, will not cease to exist and that in the end you will be just fine? You started this civilization with only the basics and the will to survive. The loss of your iPod, having to make do with fewer pairs of shoes, or choice of breakfast cereals will not make or break the human race, nor will it be the deciding factor in your ability to survive. The Sun doesn't set just because someone says it's time to; it does so because the current cycle has been completed, nothing more, nothing less. And please, do not get Me started about the all too common quotation of "death and taxes," there are many absolutes in this Universe, yes, the end of a physical cycle is one of them, taxes is most certainly not one of them.

I want you to envision a very tangible reality in which nothing is ever lost or destroyed. Can you hold it in your mind's eye? Now I ask that you paint yourself into this tapestry, this reality and by all means bring along all your loved ones, pets and close friends. Now I ask that you accelerate your perception of *linear* time to an event of when one of your loved ones becomes elderly and passes over from this reality that you have just fast forwarded into. If you truly believed what I have shared with you "that nothing is ever lost or destroyed," what do you think it would take for you to believe Me when I tell you that no one *ever* ceases to be? That in fact it is only their bodies that give out. My point here is if you each can get past the illusion of never being able to see your loved ones again and if you grasp the larger concept of living in the Now, which exists within a timeless continuum that is constantly in motion and harmoniously playing all lifetimes simultaneously then maybe, just maybe, you will understand the likelihood of your seeing your loved ones again is not only plausible, it is entirely true and well within your grasp. NIRVANA is no more than a stone's throw away. Soon, those of you who survive will know this as a certainty for you will be able to travel back and forth to there and visit some of your old friends and acquaintances. NIRVANA is as real as you or I AM. It exists on many different levels, just as the various realms and dimensions do that I spoke of earlier.

Each tiny step you take in believing in the concept of the Now brings you one step closer to actually propelling yourself out of the confines of linear time and into the vast presence of the continuum. Then you will start living in the Now. I want you to think back over the past day, week, or month. Has there not been some instance where you felt as if time had stood still, or where it had accelerated to an unnatural pace? Or course you have. Revel in your awareness, be stupefied and bewildered if you must, but I ask that you rise up to meet your Higher Self and sever your Earthly bondage issues. Believe in the unbelievable, believe in magic and by all means believe in yourself and your own abilities. The higher you raise yourself up the closer you will come to comprehending that you CAN exist in two worlds simultaneously. One world is the practical, physical, everyday world and the other is a sensuous, Spiritually satisfying realm of inner knowing, where peace, contentment and a sense of purpose prevail. I shall meet you here.

David...Have we been awaiting special spatial coordinates to arrive before we could start living in the Now or have we always had the ability to exist here?

God...You always had the ability. Many before you have walked upon the Earth Star plane and managed not to become ensnarled in the illusion. For the most part it was the simple people, those without much education other than their common sense. Remember, I have said repeatedly that the intellect is trained to believe in the illusion; do you find it surprising that Children do not know of the existence of linear time until taught by their elders the great untruth...that time exists? What they do know is that everything is happening in the moment. That is until the great lie is foisted upon them. I remind you of the animals; they exist in the Now. They would not know any other way. They eat when they are hungry, they sleep when they are ready and all of this is done by instinct. Instinct is vastly misunderstood here. It has been described as a gut feeling, yet it is the ability to not second-guess one's Self. Feel it, sense it and trust in it and you will all be better off.

David...Do you have any comments on Daylight Savings time?

God...Daylight savings time is another abomination started by those who believed they could manipulate other peoples' realities. The body goes into shock each time it has to readjust itself to fit a parameter that does not coincide with its own internal time clock. The body knows how much rest it needs, just ask it. Twice a year your entire systems are thrown out of whack until you readjust to this new schedule. Is it worth it? Can you not simply acknowledge that the days get longer in the summer and vice versa in the winter? The sky is blue, water is wet and you need oxygen to breath. Getting up in the morning and starting work when its right to do so should be as natural as knowing when to breathe.

David...If we throw away all our clocks, how will people know when to take their prescriptions?

God...My facetious friend, you know My response to that one. Happily the time is almost at an end where any of you should need to take a pill to repair something that was damaged by the same groups that caused the ailments in the first place. I will leave it at that.

God Talk 3

Life as a Morality Play

God *(received by David)* The curtain has been raised, the next act has begun and all the actors are in their designated places playing their parts. The show has started without any hiccups and the scene is set. Everywhere in the world the characters, those of the human race, are performing their parts and the show **will** continue to go on. There are many scenes that have been set in motion and have been continuously playing from the earliest beginning of the human race. Knowing the difference between right and wrong had intentionally been connected to each of your minds. Now as we approach the final curtain call it is time for you to choose how you exit. I implored you from the beginning to do the right thing for the right reason and at the same time I applauded your ingenuity for seeking new ways to express yourselves without crossing the line between decency and decadence. So when did it go wrong, when did some of you first stop believing in the inevitable, that karma would raise its head and confront you? I wonder how you would explain to others that many wait until they are on their deathbeds before they decide it might be time to do what's right and honorable. Is it fear that drives them to the edge of the moral precipice?

Teetering out there all alone can be mighty unnerving for someone who has always *looked the other way.*

I wish to speak briefly about karma for a moment, for it plays a keen role in your development individually as well as the evolvement of your species. Most of you believe karma can and will come back to bite you... eventually. That is not giving karma much credit now is it? How many of you are aware that there are good forms of karma? This is not commonly considered in your thoughts or actions. Some people find it easier to believe in the ominous force defining *their* perception of bad karma and the fear of that alone restrains them from doing anything wrong. They are not giving themselves much credit here. Fear of anything sets karma in motion and fear itself has many faces, as does Karma. Karma should be acknowledged as a stepping stone in Spiritual evolvement. I might suggest you think of Karma fondly when you do acknowledge it, then do something good and *give it some teeth.* Momentum is achieved by intent, you all should know this. Underlying intent is always the determining factor in all morality based judgment calls. Morals are instinctual... it is emotion that is tempestuous in many cases. Emotions are generally considered to be proactive; knowing when to rein them in is considered a virtue.

If life is a morality play, then why is it that not everyone is getting an "A" in this class? Could it be lack of personable responsibility? Are they taking the easy way out to avoid any confrontations? Are they simply wining and dining themselves on the elixir of life hoping they won't have to pick up the tab when they are done? My Children of this world, you need to be role models and I am asking each of you to stand up and be counted as the benevolent Gods and Goddesses you each are capable of BEING.

I feel and empathize with your frustration when you are trying to work with others and they can not begin to understand the virtues you are trying to convey to them. I applaud you for your dedication to be of service, I remind you that not everyone is ready to be enlightened; so choose your students wisely. Never let your disappointments in others impede your momentum. As I have told you many times before, some seeds take much longer to germinate and mature. Walking steadfastly forward while the rest of the world appears to be sliding backward is a sign of maturity and this can only come to pass if you yourself have personal goals and morals that you adhere to. No, perhaps yours are not the same as others and that is ok. You are all individuals and that IS something to be proud of.

We, My Star Keeper Children and I do enjoy watching movies with Celest and David. No, we do not always align with or agree with some of the subject matter, yet We understand the necessity of many people being subjected to the different connotations of the movie makers. Violence is prevalent on this world, to turn a blind eye to it would be a disservice to humanity. The time for ignoring the problems of this world and HOPING they will go away is long past. First you must recognize there is something wrong and then you must determine the best course of action to take to rectify it. Most of Earth's politicians do what they have always done, what they were trained to do, and that is to either cause a diversion to defuse a situation, or to throw money at the problem and hope the problem drops out of sight. That's like digging a mass grave, tossing in the bodies of ALL the dissenters and then filling in the gravesite. For good measure they then have "someone else" plant grass and rosebushes on the top and then conveniently forget that the dead or dying voices ever had the audacity to disagree with the murderers in the first place. When was the last time you saw one of your elected officials' role up his or her sleeves and jump in and get dirty? Do they do this when natural disasters occur or do they conveniently rationalize reasons to quarterback the situation from their armchair, back in their safe and comfortable environment? How long do you think it will be before they realize that **they** work FOR the people, not the other way around? For that matter, how long do you think it will take for the wealthy of this world to recognize the great responsibility they have, which is to use what has been *gifted* to them for humanitarian reasons? The old saying, "use it or lose it" comes to mind here. What is given can just as easily be taken away.

Thanks to the gifted people of this world who are sharing the wisdom of the Masters here, you will soon be able to appreciate the wonders of an upcoming civilization that will become a marvel of itself. For far too long the masses of this world have been morally and Spiritually depraved. They have allowed the emergence of a lower evolved species to influence their lives when all along they, YOU, have had the power to flick them away. Just your admission of this fact, the verbal acknowledgment of this fact alone would send them reeling, twisting and revolting amongst themselves. You see, they know far better than do you, that if they can not be supported by the people of this world, they cannot survive here. As I have mentioned to you in the past, they require your lack of resistance, your fears, insecurities and lackluster faith in order for them to exist. They use you, they toy with you and taunt you and you have allowed them the right to do this. A Soul in decadence can not survive in close proximity to a Soul filled with decency, no more so than a fish could survive without oxygen in the water.

The majority of the people I speak of here are the ones who have been intentionally misinformed and misdirected by their teachers, their peers and of course, the media. In earlier times it was necessary to use force to coerce people into believing that they alone held no true power. In today's current societal structure, the few can and do coerce the many by simply misrepresenting or omitting information that would be crucial to anyone who is truly trying to determine an accurate assessment of an event. If you want to believe something and you don't see others or read about others who can collaborate with you about your beliefs, then you, yourself, become a lone island. This island you find yourself to be can be isolated and subjected to ridicule if the opinions you have are expressed in an open forum. Morality is a two-way street. In one lane the traffic flows to the beat of a finely tuned orchestra complete with all the glamour and glitz some people would desire in order to feel enriched and appeased. The other lane is a lonely stretch of road, for there is little or no communication to be had with others in order to *fuel the engines*, so to speak. The first, while *appearing* to be more inviting is not in your best interests, it is however the path of least resistance. Which will you choose the high road or the moral road? Morality is not always the most popular stance to take, it is however the most beneficial to one's own Spiritual growth.

I watch in utter dismay as many of you choose to ride upon the Spiritual wave only to be knocked off because someone, somewhere, told you something that was not necessarily true. Yet you accepted what you were told as fact based and built the cornerstone of your foundation around this one lie. I ask you to confirm all the information you receive, no matter the source. Judge for yourself whether it is valid or not. If it is not then you are setting yourself up for a fall and believe Me, this abyss is not one that is easily climbed out of. We who are the watchers pay keen attention to your decisions as you enter the crossroads. It is here at the crossroads in life where life's most brilliant dramas and best made plans may be laid to rest. Choice is always relevant here, remember, it is the intent and purpose behind the choice which defines you. Life has many turns; it challenges you to better yourself *because it can.*

Life centers around morality. Take for example the moral issues of yesteryear that are still ongoing in the current timeline. We all had to bear witness to the un-holiest of holy wars and I would be amiss not to bring attention here to every religious confrontation since then. Then there are the insanely cruel acts of human trafficking on all levels. Is nothing sacred? And let us not ever forget about the Spanish inquisition, the witch trials etc. and the list goes on. Sadly, We ALL must remember the very real attempts at forcibly "breeding" out impurities in people, all accomplished under the guise of "for the common good." Now think about this for a moment, in an advanced society does any of this make any sense to you? Why is it that when something is different, or you don't understand it, you try to eradicate it, enslave it or profit from it? The people of this world who still believe that they alone are better than ANY others, are in for a rude awakening as the "useless eaters" the "second class citizens" and those commonly referred to as "the lower caste," rebel and demand equality. Citizens of planet Earth, most of you have forgotten what is truly worth fighting for. Perhaps I should have put **a price** on it so you would recognize its value. Is it gold and silver, or silky linens? In the days ahead as water becomes very scarce and the price of food outweighs that of gold and silver, what will you do to help one another? Will you continue to do as the masses have always done? I ask YOU, are you willing to go down that road or are you finally willing to take a Stand?

Being morally and ethically sound in principle when the turbulence around you suggests that adapting either a *stand and fight* stance, or perhaps alternately understanding that *engaging in a flight mode* might be simpler, is not always an easy choice and certainly not one that I can make for you. I hope you have learned your lesson of the day for you WILL need it in the days ahead, that I can guarantee.

David...Has there ever been a civilization that de-evolved as the human race has? I say "has," because I am in full awareness of what this beautiful planet has gone through. As well as all she has given up to provide us with the unique type of playing field or environments necessary to give us all the lessons we needed, so each of us could evolve individually, as well as a collective.

God...Do you mean besides human civilizations of the past?

David...Yes.

God...Of course.

David...Will we learn from our mistakes this time around?

God...Eventually. You know I do not go in for the "no pain-no gain" concept. However difficult it may be, you collectively WILL learn this time around. Consider this to be written in stone, because it is. However pleasant or painful you choose to make it, is up to each of you.

David...So you are saying that we, as a race, are at the end of a cycle?

God...At the completion of every cycle is the beginning of another one. This process never stops.

Celest...God, I understand that as each cycle ends another automatically begins in an overlaying fashion. I know that this is to ensure that nothing is lost and that many of the human race will simply leap into the next part of their reality. Those who do not will simply drop from view. However, as a race, which cycle do you see as the one that will provide the most important "endings and new beginnings?"

God...This cycle that the human race is just beginning to finish is the one that I see as the most important one. This is because without this particular cycle taking place, how could there be a better one? No one here would have anything to compare the new one to and so many would not have learned about their own foibles and their own strengths. I will leave it at that for now.

God (received by Celest) Often I hear all My Children at one time or another, wondering strange disquieting thoughts about life in general. I find it disturbing that <u>some</u> of the ones I hear thinking or verbalizing to others will state..with great authority I might add, "there is no hell; hell is here on Earth." Really now Children, this type of thinking is a disgrace to you each as Soul. "Morals and morality"....if you truly understand what those terms mean, then you are halfway there to understanding the PLAY you are each participating in. Morals themselves are sets of personal virtues, pure ideas, enhanced dreams, the desire to progress rather than regress and intrinsic worth. They function as a type of yardstick in determining how much you have relearned and how far you still have to go to get to where you should be or want to be. "Virtues" in this sense have absolutely nothing at all to do with any religious connotations. Morals themselves are dependent on the ideas, imaginations, diversity of thought patterns and Soul's abilities to recognize that incoming ideas or elongated thoughts can be either a boon or a BOOM. Well Children, I ask you all now a simple question. Do you define morals as something that is determined by the way you live your lives or are they the determining factor in Creating a pattern in your lives? I will of course not give you the answer. You may mull this one over for yourselves.

I do realize of course that many religious people believe they are very moral if they attend their churches, temples, synagogues and the like and rear their progeny to do the same. Yet, millions upon millions of these people are the very same ones who commit adultery, murder, theft and incest to name just a few invasive attacks committed by them against others. Then too there are all the men, women and sadly young Children, who are caught up in the drug-ridden cultures yet justify their actions to themselves. And justify this they do. Just ask them, they'll tell you! You are not "born into morals;" you either have them or you do not. It is all predicated upon you, as an individual, either using your true knowing of right and wrong, or not doing so. I have yet to see any profession, any field of expertise where **all** the people in those fields have morals. Yes, this is also very true sadly enough, of those who walk what they perceive as their Spiritual path.

Each person should have moral judgments; each person should understand the life they are living is the *core* of the truest morality play ever enacted on the Earth Star planet. How do you understand moral judgments when at other times I impress upon each of you never to make judgment calls upon others? Very easy to do Children. Moral judgment is simply a way of stating that some thing is very rotten to the core or very pure at heart. You are not MAKING or PASSING judgment; you are decoding an event, an issue or a person. It also always very simply clarifies what side of the coin you stand on. Those aligned with superficial people and exploitive people and the simply delusional people are not exhibiting moral judgment. They see nothing wrong with those other energies simply because they possess them themselves.

The people here on the Earth Star planet that practice autonomous life are Creating and sustaining their own personal code, this is most desirable behavior as long as it is not at the expense of others. As these people here observe the madness that is steadily increasing among the people of this world, everywhere in actual fact, they steadfastly refuse to become aligned with that madness and deplore the illusionary rhetoric these marauding people are part of. An individual's morals can alter minute by minute depending on the Spiritual fortitude of that person and the codes he or she lives by and with. When 2 or more people live together and they do not all share the same moral codes, then someone will crash and burn. Sometimes it is sheer ego alone that will keep a person in the grip of immoral codes. Other people live lives needing to always impress others with what they think they know. Their own moral codes are stunted. If you must impress someone else then it is not the other person who has the problem. It is you.

Morality itself can be seen as a personal code of conduct. Of course that is only applicable if one has a conscience. Not all My Children do, you know. They may not all be sociopathic, but you still would not want to encounter then in dark alleyways. In this particular lifetime you are each learning more and more about what SHOULD be the priorities in life. The truest test you will each undergo is how you now apply those priorities to your own belief systems. Thankfully, the expanding collective conscious is attracting more and more Souls who are Earthbound. In this manner each Soul who implements right action in conjunction with right thinking is unconsciously contributing to the collective. Just imagine for a moment how much more can and will be achieved as you turn around and initiate the movement of the conjunction consciously. What wonders We shall all behold. Children, although great chasms have become quite apparent now that **SEEM** to be separating so many people of all cultures, all races, from one another, in fact it is not. These breaks are actually showing you each the continuity of all that must change, all that needs to be revealed and understood. These chasms are a perfect example however of how certain belief systems and behavior that is unmodified must be shown to each person on the planet. If it were not for the chasms, I ask you now, how would you know? Yet, far too many of you wander around sometimes in disbelief at the variegated actions and beliefs of others. Why?

If you still were in total ignorance as you once were, you would not be able to formulate your own ideas of right and wrong, you would be incapable of arriving at a point of thought that equates with knowing that another culture, another race, may believe differently simply because that is the way of their ancestors. It has become a way of life that may stupefy you; however it does not alter the fact that this is the foundation of their beliefs. It is how they were raised. They were raised on their own ancient teachings; many of those cultures have been brutalized into remaining on the ancient course, following the ancient ways. They do not see themselves as lacking in morals, you know. Rather, they see all others who do not follow their lead, those who believe in different realities, as the true outsiders, the true enemies. These people do not even realize they are being fed un-idealistic delusional realities by the unilluminated force. Life cannot be a complete union of mind, heart and Spirit unless you follow a moral code. Think of morals as a template; it is here that you shall either grow or become stunted. It is here that life itself shall either become magnetized to you as an individual who is exhibiting a true life force, or life will become a barren wasteland for you. It will offer nothing. Sometimes not even the barest of necessities.

I admonish each of you this day to think carefully about your own life rather than another's. Decide for yourself if you wish to continue to live or if you will become one of the millions and millions of My Earthbound Children who will not survive the current and coming changes. **This is the reason I am writing this chapter in this book!** I do warn all of you now, that a life, any life experience but this one in particular, cannot salvage the mind that is filled with dross, the hearts that are black with rage and hate, or the Spirit that has become badly tarnished and deformed. Celest, are you ready for Me?

Celest... God, after that particular mouthful, or should I say "mindfull," I can only hope that I am! God, is or does each moral that is defined by the individuals' mind and Soul remain as a tangible or an intangible? Do morals themselves not only dictate the way of life that an individual may have, or are they reliant on others' thoughts? Those others may be ones who may share a symbiotic or perhaps sympathetic relationship with the individual.

God... Very good Celest, I intentionally refrained from discussing the first part of your question in this chapter because I knew these questions were already buzzing around in your mind. There are energies that are the predominant ones in every lifetime. However the dominant energies can either be enhanced or diminished by one's moral code. In this sense the dominant energies present at any given time that are in a position of elevated consciousness are then indeed tangible. Thus they can be seen by the manner in which one expresses themselves. Also in the behavior pattern and speech of a person. Yes, these energies are tangible because they have been given "form in expression." The intangible energies quantify the tangible energies because of a natural cohesiveness that each one of these energetic matters possesses. So, as one moral possessed by the individual is part of the predominant energies, the intangible ones that can be accrued through this lifetime will give more structure to the original morals. Again, think of the template I spoke of. Think how many times a template of this nature can be utilized for the betterment of the mind, body and Spirit simply because they all work in tandem.

This is also why energies that are intangible CAN become tangible as well. Understand please, there is no limit at all to how many of these morals can be birthed and then enhanced. Each moral has a "sub-moral." For instance: an individual possesses a moral of "truth at all costs." What this essentially means is that an attachment of sorts, that is perhaps truth relative only to that person rather than to other people, will have a functionality of unconsciously, consciously and Super consciously, ferreting out truth regardless of what pain or punishment may be the end result of the search. You may all think of the moral code as a house; there are many rooms in the house although only a certain number of them are considered to be the main rooms. The other rooms then would be sub-rooms. The activated morals of any person will consistently undergo a permutation in order for that person to grow in consciousness. Of course when there are no TRUE moral codes inherent in many of the individuals on the planet, then those energies that had been destined to become a vitally important aspect of the life force of those individuals wither and ultimately die.

No, morals are not reliant on the thoughts of others; each person may share a symbiotic relationship with some of the moral codes of others, however each thought pattern of each person differs in some way or another. A sympathetic relationship however just does not seem to have longevity. It simply comes and goes. There Child, have I answered your questions to your satisfaction?

Celest...You always do God, thank you.

God Talk 4

The Tyrannical nature of Evil and Fear

God (received by Celest) Although I have in the past spoken at great length on the subjects of fear and evil, I still see and hear far too many people who simply can not seem to see both those energies as the combined force they truly are. Evil is of course the opposite of good; fear is an offshoot of an energy that causes the intellect to respond in almost a kneejerk reflex. Fear can and does shake the very foundation of your life, if you allow it to. Fear is in a very real sense the antithesis of confidence and the betrayer of your weaknesses. It teaches you to give away your power, thus empowering fear. Therefore, when your intellect signals an immediate warning of a fearful situation, event, or person, a simultaneous occurrence takes place. Immediately the emotional body of the person reacts on an instinctual need to survive; which is to either fight or to run, whatever the person is most capable of doing at that moment. Fear also has an immediate effect on the adrenaline and all organs of the body. The entire circuitry necessary to maintain the life force of the body is threatened; it is compromised whether momentarily or for a longer duration of time. The brain is USUALLY the part of the body that takes longer to recover from fear because of the memory of the event.

This is the fear factor at work. It unfortunately breeds more tangible aspects of itself with every invasive incursion targeting the individuals. Fear actually promulgates itself through the simple method of repetitiveness. I told each of you long, long, ago, well before your initial descent to the Earth Star planet, that all matter, all energies possess their own indelible fingerprints. So why would anyone not understand that the fear factor of course has it own? Think about a fingerprint for a moment, please. It is a type if stain, it does not mean that they all must be perfectly round and contain whorls. It means that they leave a residue of themselves that must be eliminated if that particular fingerprint is dangerous to have. This of course is when things get a bit tricky. If people do not know they have the fear factor and what fear is then how can they eradicate it? The physical vehicle learns quickly to identify certain emotions that the flow of adrenaline is interpreting as dangerous. Adrenaline then rapidly moves through the body which causes constrictions on every possible level to the entire physical vehicle and CAN slow or temporarily freeze the thought processing. *Uncertainty, uneasiness, fearful thought waves and a sense of impending harm or doom,* are but some aspects of the thoughts and senses a person may experience at that time. The physical vehicle alerts all aspects of a human being to these understood sensations. They are only understood because they have happened before.

Eliminating fear is not easy; once a fear has been birthed the individual experiences great qualms, understandably so, of having the fear re-experienced. Physical pain produces fear, yes, but that type of pain possesses no memory to link it back to the body. You remember that a pain may have been sharp or dull and you remember that it really hurt. However, you can not recreate those sensations non-physically; you simply have memory of the unfortunate event. Only a repetition of that pain physically reminds a person that they have had it before, so they recognize it as recurring pain. To eliminate any fear, you first must confront it. In so doing you can and will understand that fear and then you will either set up a **type** of corresponding energy that understands fear and can successfully combat it, or you will need to sever it completely by denying it entrance. Either way it requires practice, dedication, determination and patience in order to root out the fear and dispose of it. If you bear in mind that fear is a conditioned response to circumstances you have seen as beyond your control, you can break the fear cycle by altering the circumstances OR by thinking of other options you can take to Create new and better circumstances.

Now evil on the other hand is the surrogate child of the Children of a lesser god. Evil is a non-evolving blob; it is a mass of congealed bloated energy containing the darkest of the darkest of unhealthy, dangerous and life threatening matter. Evil is the great parasite; yet it needs to always find hosts in order to continue to expand itself since it is unable to evolve. It may find new more scurrilous methods of projecting itself, but it is reliant on the human mind to continue to breed new clusters of itself. A person's imagination can project new forms of evil; new forms of disgusting bondage and dangerous lewdness of thought and action. So, being careful what you think is tantamount to you, yourself, not unconsciously forming new and worse forms of evil. Evil is a contagion; in one sense you may think of its toxicity in the same manner you equate with a virus. It always seeks out the people who either follow the path of least resistance in life, or the ones whose staunchness of faith and continuity of Spirit and their will to succeed in life causes them to be very, very, large targets.

It is then that evil will usually send the "come hither" command to fear in order to cause fear to come yet again and contaminate a person. My Children of this planet choose to <u>not</u> see that evil and fear can be inseparable in most cases. Children who refuse to recognize the existence of evil are easy targets for an energy they refuse to believe in. Yes, there truly are those who absolutely refuse to acknowledge the concept of evil. Needless to say that is always their undoing. There are very few individuals that have crossed over into the realm of pure evilness who can ever find their way back to goodness and wholesomeness. Those few who do however, generally have short life spans after that. Too much damage has been done to the psyche and of course the physical vehicle. Although it MAY happen that these people can leap the evil hurdles, they have still effectively set the odds against themselves. Then of course there are those people who cross over from good to evil with very little remorse or no remorse at all. They fear that if they do not cross over they will fail in whatever venture they want to accomplish. Foolish Children. They have little or no understanding that they can only fail themselves by taking such wrong actions. They have become too embroiled in their fears. They are also the ones who fear truly living **life.** In an ironic way evil unconsciously serves a purpose it never intended. Those people who can recognize evil no matter what form that energy chooses to take, seem to gain more inner strength through the sheer understanding that although they may see it for what it really is, the fact that so many, many, others can not, confirms to the people who can see, the power of evil to overwhelm the psyche of each person who falls. That period of being overwhelmed affects each person in a different way. No two methods are exactly the same. Evil seeks the vulnerabilities you have. Then of course fear steps in and begins to reside and then root itself into the body, mind and Spirit of a person. Oftentimes however, small fears first enter and then are quickly followed by the entrance of evil and larger fears.

Although fear causes a splintering within the psyche which will become deeper and more exploitive, it is evil that will attempt to break the psych into shattered pieces of itself. As this occurs all is truly lost to the individual. Damaged psyches function irrationally. In just but a short period of time it can become totally corrupted. Serious health problems always occur when the psyche arrives at this state. I ask you each to not try to mend the psyche of another person who has crossed over. It is a highly volatile situation when goodhearted people attempt to do this for another. Please remember the contagion I spoke of. Whatever your own vulnerabilities may be, they will become even greater by your associations with these other people. Evil has always had a need to survive. Only by this energetic mass's ability to survive can Souls be overcome and planets destroyed. Only in this manner can evil propagate itself. Evil however has its own vulnerability, you know. It can not survive when exposed to the Light of all Lights. All fears are centered within the mind; therefore the mind is the perfect feeding place for violence to take place. Here is the arena where Soul and mind must face each other in oftentimes **immortal** combat. Fear does not give meaning to your life; instead it gives you a life without meaning.

Evil and fear have little difficulty in locating new hosts. There are always more Souls to cull. The conjunction of evil and fear as a diabolical twosome is what in great measure has been holding you all back from being your own true selves. The media and other businesses of life only contribute to all that you have become conditioned to fear. If you can learn to remember that both fear and evil are actually obtuse, even if those two masses do not recognize this fact, then you can not fail to win against these entities. Once again I ask you to please listen to the advice I am giving you; recognition is your key to success as well as to your survival as independent, unique human beings.

Celest...Am I correct God that you have chosen to include this chapter because of the ongoing situations on the planet that have to do with planetary changes, alignments and the peoples' responses to all this happening?

God...Yes, Celest, you are correct. I had hoped that more and more people in this world would have come to better conclusions by now about how their individual roles contribute to the collective consciousness and to the continuing saga of the betterment of Terra in general. However, I am paying close attention to all those Children who have read My previous books and have seen that many of those Children have resettled themselves back on the treadmill they thought they had left. My goal in this particular book is not so much to inspire people, but to give them all the reality checks I know they need. I do not like to lose even one Soul. The vast numbers of Souls who are refusing to alter their perceptions can not assist in the betterment of the planet, nor can they function as role models for My stouthearted Children who are pursuing the path leading to a better life, in a better time. Terra is of course doing her part in shedding her skin, so to speak. She is being especially helpful in uncovering old mountain ranges beneath the waters and causing the waters to change course as well as depth.

However, it is the Children I am concerned about. Millions them still choose to toggle fear as if it were something necessary in their lives. Fears and disorganized chaos walk hand-in-hand. The fact that many of you believe that you must have disorganized chaos in your lives is appalling, to say the least. Children, I tell you each very seriously that backpedaling now simply will not do.

Celest...God, would you please explain to the readers how you feel they can best retrain their bodies in order that the bodies do not continue to react to fears? You already explained the recognition factor of evil, but perhaps a few words about this other matter would be helpful as well.

God...That is a superb suggestion, Celest. You are correct, it is timely information. Ok, your bodies always react to outside stimulus. So by nonverbally addressing your mind and your intellect you can with great effect alter certain patterns that the mind and intellect react to, thereby altering responses the physical body itself receives. IF you remember that the mind is a gigantic computer that is linked to the circuitry of the intellect, then you should be able to assess for yourself how one can commandeer the other unless you have programmed them to work together. How long it will take for each person to re-modify that union is of course up to each individual. Obviously those who have spent their entire lives in fear MAY have a most difficult task ahead of them. Even so, as the body relaxes it will take its cue from what is being broadcast to it by the mind and the intellect. Yes, Children, this takes patience and daily practice but it CAN be done.

Choose your thoughts carefully, and reaffirm positive thoughts and address what your fears were. Then inform the intellect and the mind that those fears no longer exist for you. Again, this will take practice.

Celest...God, would you please explain to the readers about the arena where mind and Soul confront one another? Also please define "immortal combat" in these instances.

God...I have explained some of the areas of dimensions and realms that exist even though they are far beyond the understanding of the average individual here. Although the mind is a part of the brain per se, all that is born into the mind as thought waves and patterns of thought that become permanent attributes or fixations and all ideas sent to mind from Soul, exist there within the physical body, but also exist in a dimension that is a type of gathering place for all those thoughts and ideas. This is also where all the ideas and thought conceptions developed by the personality itself as a result of varied events and experience in the lifetime are stored. In a manner of speaking it is a place of self-examination. It is here where so much of what each individual conceives in thought is explored by those who are the keepers of that realm. I suppose you could compare it to an off world encyclopedia. You see, this makes things so much easier for each Soul to decipher after they have transitioned from the Earth Star planet. All that each Soul accrues as new ideas, new patterns of thoughts or the acceptance of what others' thoughts may be, are scrupulously studied here by the Soul who possessed the thoughts while he or she was in mortal form.

As Soul studies all that had been previously believed or accepted, Soul then encourages whoever the life form will soon become (the soon-to-be personality) regardless of whether it will be a man or a woman, to segregate himself or herself from thoughts that had been proven to be highly detrimental in the previous life experience. In this manner Soul can encourage ItSelf to follow a proven truth and to remain aloof from the illusions of thoughts once believed and followed. Of course all this data is transmitted to each Soul Cluster who then transmits it to the main OverSoul Cluster. This is a proven method of expanding Super Consciousness by reinforcing the strengths of thoughts that can aid in Creating novel ideas and events and also provides the wherewithal to show and teach new Souls about why certain thought patterns should not be followed. It is a powerful defense system that also functions as a teaching aid.

So, when the personality begins to relate to the wrong concepts in life, Soul freely operates in a beneficial pattern by attempting to remove the wrong and dangerous ideas through a series of prophetic dreams and increased sentience. This may sound simple; however it really is not in most cases. This usually does ignite in a battle of vibrations and frequencies and for the individual who is not consciously aware of the battle, he or she may develop a type of restlessness or uneasiness. You see, millions and millions of people reincarnate here who still try to hold on to their previous misconceptions. Even though they may have "seen the Light" when they left their previous mortality, old patterns are not easy to break. Until a person has had enough of the experience, those experiences just do not stop. Many an old Soul still tries to interrupt the experience process, however if the personality is still desirous of those encounters then Soul can only go into battle. This is the simple version of those events.

Celest...Thank you God, now we can turn this over to You and David.

God (*received by David*) Those of you who are living now have an awesome responsibility here in the present to represent Me in the best fashion you can. Each one of you must find the means to distance yourself from the lunacy that has been allowed to permeate this world. To do this you will require unlimited amounts of fortitude, desire and above all, determination. When necessary you must dig deep down inside to find the strength to keep on going. You have all come too far to give up now. There is not one among you who are reading My words who should be ready to throw up your hands and give up, it is not in your nature. I have told you before, never ever give up, surrender when you must, but never give up. There are a great many of My Children in need of your strength, guidance and encouragement right now. I picked you; yes YOU, to be here now so that I could count on you when I need you most. To accomplish this I need all of you to be much stronger in your resolve to make a difference than you ever thought possible.

I want to show you a world without fear. A world where evil would be afraid to venture. I want you to see that the possibilities of this are not only real, but well within your grasp. I want to encourage you, I want to bolster your beliefs and I <u>will</u> walk side by side with you as you do this for Me. My beloveds, you are the cream of the crop; you are My front line of defense. You couldn't let Me down if you tried. My Children, let us walk together hand in hand into a valley of splendor. Let us, you and I, rebuild this world anew.

In the past many of you out of necessity have walked this world alone, now there are millions just like you. The forces have been gathered, the gauntlet which was laid to rest has once again been raised. Take pride in knowing that soon there will be no more challengers for the supremacy of this world. We (you and I) will see to that. There is only one last confrontation on the horizon. As this world continues to transform itself there will be many frightened people. You must show them the way. You must offer them your shoulder to cry on, and when necessary you must be the rock they will lean on. Can you do this for Me?

This, the final battle is not being fought over resources or lands; it is being fought in the hearts and minds of the individual. Many will stumble, others will fall. Do not be among them. The most unlikely of Spiritual Warriors will rise from the ashes and together you will banish evil from Earth with one fell swoop. Remember, you will be among the Warriors. Take pride in that. The differences that have divided you will fade away; you will find common ground which will assist you in rebuilding the human race. You will either work in concert, or you will not be here.

This world is but one of the collective of planets in this Universe. She is as unique as each of you are. Despite this uniqueness there are bonds that bind all of you together, yet many may not yet understand this. We will change that. When one planet ascends to a higher vibration it has the wondrous effect of lifting all other spheres up to another level. When a planet descends in vibration the opposite obviously occurs. This is what has been happening with the Earth Star and it is affecting the rest of the Universe. As all life everywhere is connected, this has had an adversely lingering negative effect on all the other Universes as well, parallel or not. So why am I bringing this up at this time? I wanted you to see the correlation of thought and action and the effect even the tiniest of changes has on other forms of life. I allowed this flirtation of yours with evil so that you too would know how pain and suffering can spread like a contagion. I also wanted each of you to know how good it can feel to heal a world and have it become whole once more.

Think of fear and evil as the disease they are. Diseases must be eradicated before they are allowed to spread. Never again will this world be subjected to the pain and torment she has had to endure. Never again will a species be allowed to occupy this world if that species is not Spiritually evolved. Never again will any of My Children have to leave the surface of this world and descend to the sanctuary of Middle Earth awaiting the time for the rest of the human races' ascension.

Now since David's mind is referencing what I have just said to "knowing when to walk away from people," I shall begin by saying...now is a good time to walk away from friends and loved ones that are not showing signs of a desire and intent in finding a way to move forward. It is not that you do not love them anymore; in a very real sense you are giving them the greatest gift of all by walking away and allowing *them* to question why you deemed it necessary to do so in the first place. At this unprecedented stage of the game you cannot allow them to interfere with your personal destiny. Please do not expect those that you walk away from to understand why you are doing so. This will not happen. In many cases it will be like an ugly divorce. Just keep your moral compass pointed in the direction you are going and don't look back. Take comfort in knowing that eventually they will be right where you are now and they will have to make the same difficult decisions you have had to. In all likelihood, if you continue your ascension process, the odds of you being there at that time acting as one of their Spirit Guides or mentors are quite high.

Have the tyrants exited this world? No, not all of them. Most of the remaining ones have merely polished up their acts. It is easy to see through their disguises if you look closely enough. There are many self-proclaimed philanthropists who are nothing of the sort. I spoke of evil wearing many guises, always look for the underlying intent. Ask yourself what it is that they intend to receive from their acts of kindness, learn to read between the lines. The truth will always reveal itself. My NESARA Wave will see to that.

Today, *this day*, is the beginning of a new way of life here on Earth. I encourage you to seek new ways to support your Spiritual wellbeing. Learn to sense when there is a **rift** beginning within the continuum, one that you need to be aware of. As the caretakers of this world, you are responsible for defending her from anything that goes *bump in the night* and in the daylight too. I want to assure you that My Star Keeper Children and I are doing everything We can to purge the *"Legionistic"* element from this world. Much of it has already been eradicated. It is up to each of you to keep the momentum going.

For now I need you all to remain focused on the tasks at hand. Offer clarity, wisdom and understanding to those who are in need of it. Unveil the darkness that lurks in the shadows so that it can be brought out into the Light and illuminated... and then transmute it or banish it. As I told you before your world is going through a *major transformation* and you need to do your part, and when necessary **more** than your part, in assisting her to purge herself of all that has previously been allowed. She is asking you for help, will you deny her? This is the million dollar question... is your personal wellbeing worth any more or any less than hers ever was/is? Who is more connected with MySelf? The conclusions you come to will delineate the maturity and evolutionary level you are presently on. Earlier today I watched as a butterfly fluttered over and landed upon My David-Self. Did he simply think to himself "how pretty?" No, in fact he did not. His first thought was, **"We are one, you and I."** This is not something that I can teach any of you. It must be felt from the heart.

I spend a great deal of time studying the actions of My younger Children on Earth. They are so curious about every little thing. They desire to know more; consequently they ask a lot of questions. *"Why this and why that?"* They fearlessly walk upon shaky limbs suspended over creeks with no fear of falling in, because they know they can. Where fear would cause one person to turn back, the fearless Souls venture on. My Children, you all need to reclaim your youth, I am not referring to mere physical appearance. I am speaking of what is in your heart. Remove the fears about what if or may come to pass and put on your happy faces. Sorrow has prevailed too long. Find a reason why life is worth living. Find something about life that has substance to it. There is so much left unexplored. I am not speaking of places and times. I am speaking of the unseen, that which awaits you in the Light. I want each of you to *at least once in this lifetime* feel the glowing sensation of hearing the heartbeat of a tree as it grows. Watch the aura of a hummingbird in flight. Smell the aroma of the rising Sun. Immerse yourself in the winds of change and come fly with Me. The wonders that await you are more than you could ever fathom, nor are you likely believe it at this time. *Take a deep breath of the infinite and hold it for all eternity.* Be desirous of surfing upon the sands of time and boldly walk where the timid fail to tread. This is my desire for each of you. **I want you to SEE through My eyes.** I want you to feel My compassion, I want you to share in My laughter and comfort yourself in My Eternal Love. I do not want you to be afraid of your own shadow; I want you to become one with it. It is the opposite side of you, when combined with your Spirit it makes you whole. I want you to now take a deep breath, sigh a huge sigh of relief and let go of whatever it is that ails you. Purge yourself, flush the pain and sorrow of the past away and greet the new day.

In a world without fears just imagine what you could accomplish. Imagine the mountains you could climb. Imagine a world without limits, without antiquated rules and regulations. Imagine having a life that truly means something in the greater scheme. Imagine, just simply imagine, what you could accomplish if you all worked together. I want you to envision all the colors of a rainbow, all the varied hues and sense how each of these colors feel to you. Now extend out your arms and pull these sensational colors inside of you. Hold them, feel them, play with them, love them and then when you are ready, open your arms wide and send them out into the world as if you were finally painting your masterpiece. Splash a little dash here, add a collage there, sprinkle some dust over there and continue on until you are satisfied you have made some remarkably positive changes to the world you live in. Now sit back and watch the flowers grow, watch them blossom, flourish and propagate others of their kind. Take pride in knowing that you, in the here and now, are generously contributing to the expansion of life. You are in a very real sense Creating new worlds within worlds, new civilizations, new forms of life. Now you are doing something worth doing. You are embellishing the Creative Process. You are in all regards living, breathing examples of God I AM. *Welcome to My World.*

David...You said earlier in this chapter..."You remember that a pain may have been sharp or dull and you remember that it really hurt. However, you can not recreate those sensations non-physically; you simply have memory of the unfortunate event." God, is this how you perceive our experiences, our individual lives as we continue on our Earth Star walk?

God...Absolutely. The other side of this equation I already addressed in My previous book *"Beyond the Veil~Epiphanies from God"* in the epiphany entitled "I AM."

God Talk 5

The Survival Instinct

God (*received by David*) In the beginning, the Creator and I decided it would be prudent of Us to offer as many physical and psychological challenges for a new race of beings that was at that time still to be Created, as was possible. These life forms would be known as *the human race*. Because of this decision, today you are who you are, a diverse multicultural society that is capable of such great acts of kindness. On the other side of the coin you have the propensity to be unusually cruel, even to those who love you most. We must say despite all the trials and tribulations you each have had, you exceeded our expectations by utilizing your intuit imaginations. You each wanted to explore the entire range of emotions and that you have done quite successfully, sometimes to excess. We also noted that when challenges were thrown at you to test your determination and your motives most of you met them head on. Others were not so fortunate and they were as the term goes, "mowed over." Being able to adapt and improvise has generally been your strong suit. The human species is extremely resilient; this in and of itself has been your saving grace. You all have within you the best this Universe has to offer. You have the Warrior Spirit which augments your survival instincts. You like so many other races of beings have had to learn however painfully, to control this aspect of yourself in order to maintain a harmonious balance of Spiritual Equilibrium. You also have the combined intellectual prowess of species such as the Droga and many others, and you have within your grasp the combined sentience of all the higher realms. As an added bonus you have the unconditional love and understanding of the Universe herself guiding you on. There should be nothing that can stand in your way of accomplishing anything you set your mind to, now should there?

Your survival instincts once activated are secondary to none, however I am still very concerned about the increasing numbers of My *self-proclaimed* Light-workers who are becoming complacent, if not downright lazy. I know that you are all very tired and you sincerely wish for this planetary transformation to just be done and over with. I also know you have a longing for some quiet time where you could peacefully coast through life and as the saying goes...smell the roses. **That time My dear Children is not now**. Take a breather when you need to but remember, first and foremost you have work to do, work that you each independently agreed to. The time for cruising in the comfort zone is over. You have been offered a very limited window of opportunity in this lifetime to achieve your personal and planetary goals. This is not new news, it is however a point which needs to be repeated now and again. Each of you in the days ahead will be tested, retested and if necessary tested again to make sure you are not only ready, but willing and able to continue on with the accelerated ascension pace My Beloved Terra has set for you. In the past it was you who set the pace, now you have little choice but to either keep stride with the Winds of Change, or I will graciously ask you to step aside and make way for those who can. The choice is yours; there are no penalties or demerits, only alternate routes and options that will be presented to you. You have had <u>many lifetimes</u> to hone your abilities in the pursuit of perfecting yourself and this time around I/We need you to continue to perform admirably and do your best at all times. Stop trying to seek **total** perfection, you will only be disappointed. Personally, I believe you are all perfect in every given moment, so do the best you can, that is all that is being asked of you. This world is going to keep on churning, turning and twisting and those of you who can swiftly adapt to her new frequency and range of motion will prevail.

Much of the scientific community will attempt to rationalize all that they do not understand about what is currently and unstoppably underway on the planetary scene and then try to formulate that rationalization into a nice neat little box, in most cases they will fail. How can they understand? They do not know what you know; they have never been down this road before, most certainly not in Earth's current timeline. The inflexibility of the trained intellect will be their undoing. Leap beyond the confines of logic, logic is basic 1st, 2nd and 3rd dimensional processing, nothing more. You have computers now that reach well beyond that level of comprehension. You who are in tune with your Spirit Guides and are listening to your Soul Voice and are keeping abreast with the timely messages My Children and I are sharing with you, are well-versed in "Spirit Talk" and *adequately prepared* to remain consistently in the flow with these changes. Because you have this vantage point you understand what must be allowed to take place in order for the human race to continue to evolve. As your reward for paying attention you are being given advance knowledge of shifts within the continuum as they pertain to this world and all of you. Use this knowledge wisely, for to have this gift and ignore it will be fatal to each of you.

The survival instinct among those who consider themselves religious is quite strong. They will attempt to keep the illusion going for as long as they can, however their attempts will be futile. Anything that is not securely rooted in a sound Spiritual base **will** cease to be. These Souls have precious little time to search within their hearts and to realize that My Love for each of them does not come with conditions. I love each and every one equally, how could I not? Each of you is an aspect of MySelf, as I have told you many times before. My connection to each of you resides in the heart and is expressed at Soul level and this My dear Children is where you must maintain your center and what you should focus on. Self-examination of the journey each of you has taken during the duration of this present lifetime holds the keys of understanding to where it is you will be going from here. Each time you have paused in a new location you have been given a new set of instructions on how and where to precede from there. You are always given signs when the next step of your journey is about to begin. Heed these signs well, for they will navigate you safely through, around and when necessary, over the obstacles which yet lie in wait. Your finely honed instincts will warn you of any impending dangers. They will also alert you to where and when to look for your next replenishment stop. I am offering to each of you some very important guidelines for you to follow. In times past you have chosen freely to ignore these morsels of wisdom My other Children and I have offered to you. NOW is not the time to do so. Do not stray off course, the path which lies before you is not written in stone. It WAS written by your hand, from the blood, the sweat and the tears you shed lifetime after lifetime in order to get you to where you are now. Please, do not squander the precious time you have allotted for yourself to achieve your goals. Follow the guidance of your Spirit Guides; they are doing their best to keep you on the path which you yourself laid out ahead of time. If you do you WILL exceed your own expectations of what you set in motion for yourself in this lifetime.

Now Children, listen to Me please. I have tried to make your lives as pleasurable as I possibly could, while in no way compromising the lessons each of you must undertake. I gave you a good mind, a great body to service your needs; I gave you an intellect which you could train as you saw fit. I blessed you with survival instincts to guide you when the need arose. I sent you to this world so you could experience all that it is you desired. I even allowed you to stop believing in Me if it helped you to temporarily see clearly through the fog that descended upon this world. Far too many of you have lost the will, the enthusiasm to live. You have forgotten what it feels like to find joy and happiness in every moment, to be thrilled with every little thing. I ask you to not merely be alive... but to be living. My Children, when did you first notice that society was shaping who you were instead of you defining your existence? If I strip away all your comforts and toss you back into the Stone Age would you then cherish all that you have, or would you mourn what it is you believe you have lost? What will it take for you love one another? What will it take for you to believe that you are special, but not any more so than any other? I have said before "that to err is human," whatever happened to *live* and *let life happen*? At what point did you stop caring for one another? At what point did you stop believing that you could do anything that you set your heart to? It certainly wasn't because I did not give you enough chances. I speak to you in this moment as I do because I see so many of you going through the motions of living life. You can fool the naïve around you, you can not fool Me, I know you better than that. Who am I speaking to here? You decide if it is you. Now let us move on.

Your survival instincts for this current century must be altered from an "eat or be eaten" attitude to one which defines what is best for everyone. You must not allow your petty differences to divide you into opposing camps. You must find a way to work together for the common good or else you will not survive. Survivalists will draw from many elements. "Elements" being defined as the forces of nature; whether they are from the Spirit World or on the physical plane. The teachers will make their presences known here in order to lend a helping hand in organizing your options.

Listen to them well for they are all handpicked by MySelf for their ingenuity and expertise. I know you all look forward to the time when guns are no longer needed for self-protection or for the gathering of foodstuffs. Now is not that time. The gatherers among you will need to provide for those who are not capable of doing so for themselves. The protectors amongst you will need to be ever vigilant and keep an eye out for those who still cling to the old ways. Be forewarned; the gladiators of yesteryear will resurface as the weak-minded congregate together as their only perceived means of survival. They will reach out and try to destroy what you have begun to build. Do not let them. No, killing another human being is never a good thing. This does not mean you cannot utilize other means as a way to keep them from infringing upon your Sacred space. Be Creative and use what you have learned along the way.

I would like to shift gears here for a moment to remind each of you how deeply ingrained the survival instinct has become for this world herself. Had she not been willing to keep up the good fight for her own survival the planetary changes you are currently undergoing would seem trite and blasé compared to what could have been. Please keep this in mind. We are all doing what we can, when we can, when we are permitted to, to soften or alleviate the harshness, the pain, suffering and anguish that was about to bear down mightily upon all of you. I could you give you a graphic description of what was about to come to pass because I have seen it, however I would rather not. Suffice it to say, you should all feel *extremely blessed* to have this second chance. This world will no longer <u>suffer fools gladly</u>.

In the coming years many of your scientists and other individuals who had been so gullible, as well as those who have held sway over what has been done to this world, will bow their heads in shame of what they contributed to. It is not that they didn't know better, most of them were paid extremely well to ignore their commonsense and chose to try to manipulate what had already been perfected by the best scientific minds this and other Universes had to offer. What am I speaking of? Everything from the air you breathe, the food you eat, even the animals We provided for you. Why did they play with perfection? Simply put, *because they could*. Does it make it right? Absolutely not. Fortunately for you, what has been done can be undone, sadly though not without a few casualties along the way. I will speak more on this later.

The tendency of most human beings is to act first and evaluate later. People of this world, the true colors which delineate the evolutionary level of individuals mixed with the full gamut of emotions are bubbling to the surface of everyone who is not Spiritually focused and in harmony with their own Life Force. So I caution you to choose your words carefully, avoid unnecessary body language that may be mistakenly interpreted as threatening in any way. Many of those that you are dealing with may be quick to respond to anything that may rub them the wrong way. Consequently you may become the target of their insecurities and uncertainties. The Children of this world who are not *in the know* are trying desperately to hold onto their sanity. They are quick to anger and slow to cool down. So evaluate your options, choose your words carefully and avoid confrontations which may become violent. Learn when to walk away, learn when to listen and make mental notes of all you hear. There will be a great many people who will transition from this lifetime who will be caught in the crossfire, try not to be one of them.

I caution you, be ever mindful of your surroundings at all times. You will be bearing witness to untold of amounts of irrational, unpredictable behaviors. Finely tune into your survival instincts; also tune into the instincts of those of the animal species. Some will guide you and protect you, others will not, so use discernment at all times. Those animals that are not being well provided for may just be inclined to reach out and attack you even though you do nothing to provoke them. This **is not** an instinctual response; it is a learned response, one which is in direct correlation with their most basic survival instincts. The needs and desires of the people for more than a while now have been seriously infringing upon the domains of animal kingdoms. The human race has not lost the knowledge of co-existence; rather it has ignored its ability to coexist peacefully. (*David*)...A song lyric is coming into my mind "*so they paved paradise and put up a parking lot.*" **God continue**s...As the exodus from the populated areas into the rural environments increases the animal habitats will become increasingly smaller. Do what you can to protect the wetlands, the forests and start planting food-bearing bushes in the wild. Each small effort you put forth will be amplified *tenfold* in the continuum.

To each of My Children I now offer unto you a challenge. I challenge you to do better than your predecessors. I challenge you to usher in the continuum and the continuance of the Golden Now with a bang, as the old way of life is left behind without a whimper. This world demands it of you, there are no more expectations. When you look in the mirror tomorrow let the person looking back at you nod with pride and admiration for a job well done. I will end this now, questions anyone?

David...You spoke earlier of the environment, in truth, how fragile is it?

God...Extremely, there is a delicate balancing act always in motion within nature herself. This world, those of the Devic Kingdom, the Spirits which preside over the Environment, all play a keen role in the preservation of this world. As you look out in horror as the fires rage around this world know this, where you see only destruction, **I** see a new beginning. I ask you to pray for the little ones whose immune systems have been compromised. Pray for the bats and the bees. Without them you will cease to be. Pray for the oceans; they are gasping for breath because of all the invasive toxicities and the other injustices done to them. Pray for the rivers to run clean. Your aquifers are being depleted and those that are not are becoming filled with contaminants. Start using natural fertilizers to replenish the soil. Let the land rest, rotate your crops, give back to the Earth in thanks for all which She has supplied for you. Be humble and appreciative My Children. *For that which has been so freely given can just as easily be taken away.*

David...I know this is off subject but what do you think about the new telescope being built which is to replace the Hubble?

God...they will find that it is not needed and I will tell you why. In the not so distant future, My Star Keeper Children will be introducing technologies which will make the lenses of today obsolete. In addition, the human race will once again start utilizing their other senses and exploration will be done in the heart, mind and Soul through the optimization of *the Third Eye.* I will speak more on this subject in My upcoming books.

God *(received by Celest)* When the Creator and the Creation Processing decided to expand all forms, all levels, all degrees, of not only their own consciousness, but to Create a viable Super Consciousness for every life form to be Created, they did so by providing an all inclusive cyclic motion. This movement or motion would be in great measure responsible for maintaining the stability of itself in order to be a formidable force providing information that would contribute to the life force of every life form. This cyclic energy would continually work in harmony with the mind, heart and Spirit of the human species of life and all other life species. It was foreseen that life forms needed a type of contingency plan; one that was purposely designed to serve as a method of warning, as well as one necessary to maintain a cohesiveness that would serve to keep the physical vehicles alive as long as possible. "As possible" means as long as the designated timeline for that individual or clusters of individuals was destined, or in some cases, predestined to be. The term, "cyclic" is the one I have chosen to use because it impartially points out the type of action required by this energy to take and the fact that it needs to remain as a constant force while dispensing at certain times, the energetic action needed to remain part of the defense system. This mote of energy was embellished with even tinier sensors; these sensors contained a vast amount of source matter or "feelers" that could assist in detecting incoming or impending physical danger and possible death. Think of My centipede Children; think of how easily their little selves can twist and turn and how they use the many segments of their bodies, and their many legs, their "little antennas" to correctly gauge time, distance, foundations and so forth. In a sense, this is how you may think of the motes of energy I am speaking of. Not that they look much like My centipede Children. No doubt there are many of you who are glad of that!

This was to be a simple offering to all life forms. Although once the older, much more mature ancient civilizations living in other Universes evolved to such a state that they no longer needed this modality, then that small life force energy was removed from these other races, these other civilizations. That having been said I can tell you that at this point in spatial understanding there are no plans to remove it from human beings. Especially not at this time. Although I heartily agreed with both the Creator and the Creative Processing about the necessity of including this energy within the matrix of the minds and nervous systems of all life forms on Earth, We will all be very happy when the timeline arrives when it will no longer be needed. It is not that it will be considered obsolete; it simply will no longer be part of the evolved life forms who will INHERIT the Earth Star planet. Although it is true that biological necessities rely on this energy matter to further form and elongate this mass, the fact remains that from the moment you birth into human existence by whatever manner, you have it too. *An instinct is an expression of a formation of thought that is transferred into a type of sentience and action.*

Primal instinct was and still is predicated upon the ability for a person or animal to survive in order to reproduce physically or to "survive"- remain alive. Many ancient civilizations that were of this planet did learn consciously for the most part, to live outside of the confines of the instinct itself. This happened simply because they had left naiveté behind them and they grew in confidence. There were actually scant periods when clusters of people could live in harmony. Until of course greed and the ill-begotten dark lords changed the people. All humans here proceeded during a brief period of the ancient Atlantean times to follow the dictums of the Creative processing. However, Atlantis and other ancient civilizations were a type of testing ground. It was when technology that had been gifted to them by My Star Keeper races began to be abused through the process of having technology overwhelm peoples' minds that the learning arc was severed. Instead it was in fact the turning point in Atlantean history. *The people forgot their place in the Universe.* Competition that had never occurred before in Atlantis was birthed. Violence was its byproduct.

The survival instinct returned to the people; albeit too late for nearly all of them. Those small numbers who escaped Atlantis discovered that their instinct had returned even though it had lain in a dormant state for a very long time. They relearned the need for using it and they depended upon this type of "radar" to assist them on their journey. Today, the ability to live unimpeded by violent circumstances is almost unheard of. This instinct however is not based on any fear, although many people believe this to be true. Rather it is energy that is based on the biological and mental sentience that each body has. Housed within the brain it still functions as the "catalyst of necessity. " My animal Children of course now all possess this precursor of trouble. This has of course been necessary because animals have for centuries now, lived in distrust of My Earthbound Children as well as of other life forms. How can they not? Although there is yet another planet so much like Earth where the Children who inhabit that orb absolutely must have this catalyst, that planet is actually in an even lower based dimension than your former third dimension. Scary thought, is it not!

An interesting factor of how this instinct impacts on cultures is that all cultures have an inherent fear that their race, way of life and their own lineage will be lost forever if they do not continually have children. Their fears are a combination of a very deep need to be remembered, thus the fear of total alienation and annihilation pursues them. Although I am sorry that they believe that, this instinct can not in any way be considered the culprit in these cases. Indeed as My NESARA Child continues wielding her swath of truth and freedom for all, all who will be left that is, the survival instinct will become less and less noticeable among any of the life forms here. Until that finale, the gridline intersection of the climax of NESARA arrives; yes, it would be wise to follow what some of you refer to as "my gut instinct." Although the gut is not really the proper placement for this catalyst, as long as people here remember to follow through and be aware that each step taken in progressive fashion lessens the need for the instinct to remain, then all will succeed...in spite of themselves.

Celest...God, are you telling the readers that this instinct that is so precious and so intangible is also an elusive energy? "Elusive" in the sense that it is so seldom understood. And what about young Children, what about their survival instinct?

God...Well Celest, in some ways yes, it could be considered to be elusive. It does not require a microscope to know that you have it; it is intangible in a way simply because it can not be seen, but it can be sensed. Logic decrees that people need proof of the existence of anything outside of their scope of "knowing." However, even logic can not defy the reality of the biological expressions that an individual feels, experiences, or thinks about when being threatened. Many psychiatrists and psychologists like to make the implication that what is known as the survival instinct is merely a reaction to unfavorable circumstances predicated upon the fear of the unknown. For reasons known only to them, these doctors of the mind feel it necessary to impugn these experiences their patients have, until of course it happens to them as well. As far as this instinct being seldom understood is concerned, it is difficult for many people to believe in something that they feel they have no control over.

Let's say a person has always been physically threatened by another person. The victim in that instance will continue to have the feeling of dread and the need to protect himself until such time the person posing the threats has been removed. After that, the memory may remain of what had previously occurred but it will dim, for the instinct no longer perceives the other person as the threat. As far as young Children are concerned; they are born with the dormant instinct in place. It is only as they gather life experience from those who rear them that they begin to learn fear and exercise caution in order to protect their lives. Once that need for life protection clicks into place, that survival instinct will remain with them to one degree or another for the duration of their physical lives.

Celest...Ok God, what am I missing here? Please tell us why you chose this chapter for your book. You are up to something aren't you?

God...I suppose I should ask you to define, "up to something." However.....on the conscious level Celest, you are missing the rather quaint and subtle warning I am giving to the readers. On the Super Conscious level Celest...**you knew this was coming.** There are times when I choose to alert My Children to upcoming situations by merely sending them some information relative to certain events that have already transpired in their lives. This time is no different; yet in another sense it is very different. Children, I am ringing the warning bell! There are currently world events forming that will be unstoppable. They will result in a great loss of available foodstuffs for millions of people. The droughts and floods alike will simply make it impossible for people to rely on others **as they are used to doing.** It is time for people to develop self-reliance. The survival instinct will be ringing many bells, Celest. It will warn people in advance through sheer sentience if necessary, it will insist on certain measures to be undertaken in order for people to survive that time period.

The greatest challenge here then is for the people to pay attention and perform the tasks that are needed to fill hungry bellies. THIS is why I am writing this chapter. Now, it is up to them. I have educated their realities.

Celest...Thank you, God.

God Talk 6

Planetary Consciousness and Brushes of Life

God*(received by Celest)* I have decided to speak a bit more about planetary consciousness and the import it has on all planets, all worlds everywhere, at all times. Although I am fully aware that not all people on the Earth Star planet are willing to concede that their own actions and thoughts can either negate a bad circumstance before it has had a chance to begin, or that they can Create better circumstances that would affect this planet and every human being who lives here. Not everyone understands that through the process of Creating a bucolic personal environment, even if it is only living in your mind's eye, you are IN FACT Creating your own brilliant future rather than the dubious futures that are awaiting many other people. This planet turns and realigns herself as a direct response to all that you do, say and feel. For so many millennia she has been responding to the horrendous conduct of My Earthbound Children. Even though she has had need to replenish all waterways and mountain ranges and so forth in the past, until recently she has never done so at any cost to you. That was then, this is NOW.

My Terra Child, although splendid in her own right, requires a type of replenishment that gives much more meaning to her life. Terra, just as all worlds in all Universes, retains residual effects of her own birth Creation derived from the matrix of the Creation Processing. Each world just as each evolved Universe, should always live as a convivial monad. Each of these worlds and Universes are in great measure macrocosms of themselves. Any one world, any one Universe, can experience certain healthy or unhealthy circumstances at one time or another, whether the circumstances are environmentally enhanced or a collective degradation of the enslavement of thought and energetic matter. Those worlds and Universes learn from the experiences of the planet undergoing duress as a result of the machinations of its inhabitants. They also learn from the Godlike integration of the inhabitants on other worlds. The worlds and the Universes use their sentience and their knowing and then take whatever appropriate action they deem necessary to ensure their own survival, with or without the inhabitants. It is true that you are what you think, so what does that statement tell you about your own personal world and the ominous or prophetic significance of your world affecting all other worlds? Those Children who have chosen to remain in the state of mind of megalomania can do nothing to affect the Earth Star world in any positive fashion. Yet they can and do act as powerful symbols of what <u>not</u> to do. If I told you that you who are the goodhearted Souls undergo a certain period of life where you conform to a type of deciduous energy, would you understand this? Yet, it is in every stage of your development both as a collective species as well as individuals, that you shed preconceived ideas, beliefs, thought waves and thought patterns that are in direct contrast to what you have at that time brought into your lives. With the shedding there must always be new growth of untainted and more evolved energies. This happens both collectively and individually yes, however, the collective must be dependent upon the individuals before there can be a collective, do you see? The shedding of skin is not a new concept; however few among you realize that this is what you yourselves do, but you actually do so mentally, emotionally and Spiritually. This is also when you are undergoing a permutation that permits you to more freely live as "God I AM." This dear Souls, is how grand changes are enacted on a planetary level. What must take place as "planetary," also must take place in the physicality of the dominant life species on this or any other planet or plane of thought. Millions and millions of Souls live innumerable lifetimes without having a life. This is really unacceptable behavior, you know. Millions of others seem as though they expect life to come barreling down the chimney with large bags of presents in tow. Really now, these people may not truly be addlepated, but their behavior is!

Life is its own canvas; it will remain blank until such time that the artist conceives an image of what he may want to see, thereby bringing the picture to life. Or if there is no image that the artist is truly drawn to, he may just throw some splashes of color on the canvas. In the latter case, that may be all he will ever receive from life. Life will always give you what you deserve, for life sees you as a Soul walking in physicality. Life grades you, you know. Life is neutral; it does not formulate any judgment calls on anyone. However, that having been said, I shall tell you that life has an unbroken track record of always knowing what is right, what is acceptable and what is not. Life does not wait for anyone to change; YET it can assist a person in changing when life is positive that the person will do so and has no hidden agendas. Life is not a cacophony designed to dull your senses or to cause you unpleasantness. Life is an elaborate composition of grand proportions composed of variegated elements. Color and vibration are but two of the many ones that reside in life. Life is an awesome event; although for those who simply refuse to have a life, it is an awful event.

So it is that as coup is counted and the numerical factors and possibilities and probable considerations take place, this world knows better and better how many people here will continue on and share her life with her. Planetary consciousness is a continuous evolving force; one that can not be stopped. This type of consciousness is in the greater sense, invincible. It is not muted or gray, nor does it contain hidden agendas. This type of consciousness is always in activated form. This consciousness hosts magnificent colors, hues of unbelievable beauty and harmony. It is of course a slow moving force simply because so many worlds, so many Universes contribute to this mass. This consciousness is not reliant on the consciousness of each of the other planets. However, because each planet's awareness, each planet's perceptions contain so much pure energy it is possible for each planet to not merely share the consciousness, one with the other, but to contribute to each other as well. People here on the Earth Star planet who feel as though they have been cheated by life do not really know what life is about. If you do not understand something, then how can you make any rash decisions about what you do not know anyway? Now, more than at any other time in the history of this planet, you should each be focused on a life well lived. It is by doing so that you acknowledge on all levels that you have the deepest appreciation for life regardless of what tumultuous situations are ongoing here on Terra.

It is here, when you enter that state of mind, that you will realize that perfection is not to be found on Earth. Yet, perfection CAN exist in your mind. Children, each and every time you can hold a good thought, each and every time you learn to expand upon that thought in order to bring good things to fruition, you ARE a contributing force in planetary consciousness, rather than a constricting factor. Each time a butterfly, a bird or a small child finds you and sends you good thoughts you are coloring your own perfected state of self with all the prisms of this Universe. You are embellishing the coloration simply by relishing life and honoring life by living it to the best of your ability. I can ask for nothing more than that. Invite life in; life will answer so quickly and so passionately that you will feel the difference. Use bold and bright colors in determining your future; for your future will be the planetary consciousness continual evolving to a higher more refined form of itself. As for all those others who have no colors, no tools to bring life to them, I can only say that their deep desire to leave this place will take place. I will tell you nothing more than that.

*Celest...*How long has there been planetary consciousness, God? What about life forms here on this planet that are of the animal world, would you please touch on that matter as well?

God...Planetary consciousness has been as long as there has been a Creation process. Its gestation was at first as a small but powerful **seed** of an energy that was yet to mature, to be. As the seed grew in proper proportion and in alignment with the Creation of each new world, each new Universe, it then began to harvest all the most idealistic and Spiritual thought waves and thought forms from each new orb. Idealism was a perpetual motion concept then. All worlds have at one time or another hosted some of the most idealistic civilizations you can imagine. Consciousness is a state of awareness; so the term "planetary" applied to the term "consciousness" clearly delineates that this energy must be a term applicable to all planets. All planets MAY share a certain stage and level of awareness with some other planets, so overall the consciousness we are speaking of is the centralized host that has gathered all the most pertinent knowledge of the states of the Souls overall. Again I say, it is the state of the combined Soul force that is a determining factor in the consciousness of a planet. The Creator Force in His infinite wisdom demanded that this consciousness always be used as a meter, a monitor, to adjudge the progress or regression of a world's inhabitants.

Humans were not the first species of life We Created here, you know. We brought in life forms that fly, swim in the waterways, crawl on landmasses and those who have more than two legs. The majority of animal life you know about on Earth today, were Creations from other worlds, many of them are Star Keeper animal life species as well. This is also true of the flora and fauna for example. We chose to beautify Terra in every way possible, thus allowing her to further enhance her own life in any manner she sought. Many of your life forms here as I said, are Star Keepers. Perhaps you should **all** remember that before you decide to eat whale. All life forms that predated the arrival of the human races entered into this dimension with all their sentience intact. Each of those species has its own Guardian Spirit who oversees the behavior and the evolution of their charges. Planetary consciousness does but of course also impact on all these species of life as well. These other life forms contribute greatly to the harmonious accord of the greater consciousness. Even though My Earthbound life forms that are not human have suffered greatly at the hands of humanity, they all live in **the NOW.** Furthermore, I am quite pleased to tell you that none of My animal or plant life are atheists.

Celest...All right God, thank you. I will go and eat a peanut butter sandwich now.

God (received by David) As the bells toll ushering in the midnight hour this world will begin anew. What was once lost will be found again. What was depleted will be replenished. This world, using all her sentient abilities will call forth all the magical properties she was originally blessed with. Her voice will be clearly heard in the subconscious of your minds. The connection that has been severed will be rekindled. Her connection with All That Is will grow stronger as each of you armed with purpose and intent reinforce your connection with her. In the past you have come close to finding the true meaning to life. It will now and forevermore become clearly defined. My voice will ring loudly for all the world to hear; even those with doubts will have their fears laid to rest. Children, you will breathe new life into this world as she gently brushes away your tears, and you will gladly dry hers. Tears of sadness will be turned to tears of joy. Ah, what a sight that will be.

This world, as much as she has tried to maintain a continuity of expression with you all, had lost her connection with the human race as a whole. We watched in dismay as her physical body plunged further into the abyss of darkness which was allowed to permeate her surface. As the centuries passed the repetitious death and destruction began to takes its toll. Every once in awhile a culture would emerge, a leader amongst them would arrive, one that spoke of the unbreakable connection which existed that bound all life together as one. Pockets of light would begin to emerge so the beacons of remembrances could be reignited. The lighthouses which once lay dormant in the hearts of men were relit, sending out a call for the reunification process to begin anew. These times I speak of were many; yet still the darkness grew. The waning light grew even dimmer as the wedge which separated the two of you (the human and the planet) was plunged deeper into the recesses of the heart. My beloveds, you know of what I speak, for you were there. My teachers would walk this world spreading the seeds of truth for all who were receptive to hear. The distortion which previously existed was ripped away for a brief moment leaving only clarity of thought. For a nanosecond the masculine and feminine energies merged as one and the heralding beacons would once again be lit, sending out the message that someone extraordinary was here. This message received was relayed throughout the galaxy, announcing that a new sentience had emerged. The darkness which had invaded this world knew when this had occurred and it would come forth and do its best to put out the fire. What could not be extinguished was the mote of energy which was ignited within the hearts of man. It spoke of truth, of purpose, of a grand design. It spoke of reason in a world that lost all of its sanity. The world rejoiced, the time it had long awaited was finally here. But alas, through fear of persecution the messenger was *permanently* dispatched and the connection was severed once again.

You, the children of Earth have so many times come so close to finding your rhythm with this world. Time and time again you would feel her stride quicken in anticipation... only to lose the beat. It has happened before and it is happening again here in the present. I encourage you to tune into that rhythm, sense your own heartbeat and then find the beat that unites yourself with that of this world's. Consciousness exists on many levels; the most basic is channeled through love. Send out those tendrils of yours in search of The Source. The Source awaits you. It cannot be denied.

Now that I have your attention, We, you and I, shall ponder upon the many questions which are so prevalent within your hearts and minds. This world was Created for Souls *like* you, as you were Created to be a part of her. Your roles as caretakers are simple. Protect the motherland at all costs. You **will** reincarnate and be once more, she will not. If you have to do without in order for her to heal then I ask you do so. Her needs at this time outweigh yours. At this juncture in human evolution your needs are secondary to the one that gives you life. Take a moment and think about this, for it is very important.

I want you to know that this world, she as Soul, is on an evolutionary level far above what your perceptions of her may be. No longer will she be ignored. With all her encounters *with all of you* since her tenure began **as this world,** she has had the honor and privilege to learn from all of you. Her accrued knowledge places her level of wisdom far above that of any of you. Do not doubt this. Worlds are blessed this way, what may take you lifetimes to learn, they learn in an instant. We invite you to try for just a brief time to put yourself into her shoes, if but only for a moment. Assume a detached position and look down upon your fellow man. I encourage you to quickly scan back through your history with eyes wide open. What stands out the most? Do you see repetition, cruelty, suffering and pain? Or do you see comradeship, serenity, harmony and peace? Do you see balance or are the scales of justice merely swaying in the breeze? You demand justice when you have been wronged, should the Earth herself demand the same? What would it take to right all the wrongs? Can YOU turn back time?

I make these points in hopes of reaching that part of you which can still feel, that can still care about something, *anything*, for someone other than yourself. Whether you like being dependent upon one another or not, you ALL depend, consciously or not, on this world. Care for her as you would a child, or honor her by showing her respect as you would any Elder of your tribe. It matters naught which you choose as long as you do one or the other... and soon. Today would be good. You may think I am being uncharacteristically harsh, but I want to remind you of something that you still may be too close to see. The average human being is spoiled, self-centered and has an extremely bad case of tunnel vision when it comes to anything that does not affect them personally. You have been conditioned to think and respond that way. You have been taught to look the other way; to hear, but not really listen. There is more going on than meets the eye. Step back and see, the worse that can happen is you might have an intimately personal brush with life.

Today, for many of you, is the first day of the beginning of your introduction into living in the NOW. From this moment on, if you so choose, you may start living without the presence of time in your daily routines. What this means to each of you who choose this option and yes, this is a choice, is that you will be among the first to live outside the "norm." You will find that as you embrace this *true* reality, life will become much simpler. You may also find that your sentience level which **is** directly connected to the planetary consciousness, will escalate, unify and realign with Terra's beat. As this occurs you may also find that your feelings and emotions may become more open and expressive. Be emotional, cry when you feel like crying, and laugh out loud if the mood strikes you, *and pray that it strikes often.* Allow yourself to feel impassioned by this world and all who reside upon her. The more you practice this exercise the more you will find that your minds will open up and Universal Truths will suddenly become ever so apparent to you. You will suddenly "just know" what is happening, why it is and where certain events may lead to. This is your clairsentience opening up; this IS what it feels like to be living in a higher vibration. You will feel your bodies changing; they will become more sensitive to everything from the food you digest to the tiny little particles of hair on your arms and legs. For those of you who have yet to experience the feeling of "pain" when your hair follicles become super sensitive *you are* in for a treat, ask anyone who has gone through this transition. As I have spoken of earlier in my "Letters from God" series, I have presented you with the <u>cure</u> to moving through transitions as painlessly as possible. It would behoove you to revisit these and chalk them down in your memory files for use when you find yourself *changing.* As you move through the awakening process you will feel the sensations of being one with all things. Explore this new reality, leave no stone unturned. You are the first of this new generation to experience this level of awareness. You *can* thank Terra for this. It is you who must be ready to guide others and remove the fear factor as they too experience these sometimes not so subtle, *physical and Spiritual* changes.

I will move on shortly to the question part of this narrative, in the meantime I just want to remind you, *that not everything is as it seems*. Before making judgment calls pause and take time to evaluate your first impressions. There are *slight of hand* maneuverings used by those still on Earth for the purpose of keeping you off-balance. Sometimes your Guides will do the same thing just to see if you are paying attention. Take nothing as an absolute; everything can be altered by thought, intent and desire. One person can make a big difference. Two or more when unified in thought can move mountains. This world alters with your every thought and action. Pick up your brushes now My Children, let your Soul Voice guide your hand and let's start breathing some new life into those dimly lit areas of this world, by **infusing** life into the picture. What was once dark and dismal can instantaneously be transformed into one of the most desirable places to be. All because **you** took the time, and had the desire and had the audacity to view it that way.

David...Are there direct correlations between near death experiences and the awakening process for those who some of us refer to as the "walking asleep?"

God...There are many reasons for near death experiences. Some just happen, wrong place...right time. Others have them because they need them. Liken it to a wakeup call from the motel desk clerk only with a higher purpose. In your Soul contracts you chose what your journey was to entail throughout a lifetime. You chose to allow yourself to go through life, until a predetermined gridline intersected, without any conscious memory of who you *were,* why you were *here* and what your purpose for *being* is. Many choose the near death experience as an abrupt wakeup call rather than choosing to have an alarm going off in their head, which they may or may not choose to ignore. During a near death experience many Souls receive the much needed break from the physical realm *just long enough* to let go of their Earthly bonds and rekindle their relationship with Soul. This is also the time determined by pre-birth agreements when many Soul exchanges take place. This is commonly how those known as walk-ins enter the physical realm. Other Souls when having a near death experience are catapulted at a high rate of speed into realms and dimensions far above that which is known on Earth. When they return to this dimension they carry with them their awareness of higher realms. These ones typically end up walking away from their previous existence because it no longer holds meaning for them and they begin to teach what they know to be true. Some of these teachers I spoke of earlier in My session with David.

David...So why do some people have numerous NDE's during the course of one lifetime?

God...Why not? There are many reasons for this; the most likely is that these individuals are the ones who are destined to make great changes and most go on to be teachers. These Souls are being targeted by the unenlightened ones for what they know, or for what they are predestined to do. The lesser evolved ones do not like change; if everything remains the same then the rules never change. This of course cannot be allowed. Throughout all the Universes the only Constant *is* change. Nothing ever remains the same; you can thank God (Me) for that one. Tell Me and answer Me honestly, would any of you want to go through the motions of life where everything always remained the same, like watching a really bad rerun on your television over and over and over and over again? Next.

David...So a planet is a live sentient Being just as each of us is. So *who* paired each species up with each planet, is it random, does it pertain to evolutionary status, or is there always a Divine plan?

God....David, are you baiting Me? (*God Smiles*) I see in your mind that you are thinking of days long past when the unicorns roamed this world, the Sasquatch people walked among the other races and the time long before *the others* descended into Middle Earth to escape the madness here on the surface. This world as I have spoken of before *is* MY World. It was a testing ground of sorts; but more than that it was to be a place where Souls from many worlds and dimensions could get a taste of what living a physical life was like, while simultaneously being able to benefit from the wisdom and expertise of those from the Spirit world, as well as those others who I fondly refer to as the "Star Keepers." Yes, each world was designed to be a certain way and for specific life forms who would then inhabit them. As you know, evolution has its own way of playing its hand. Planets evolve; life forms evolve, other species are introduced through the selection process of My Star Keeper Children, ALWAYS with the approval of the respective Universe's High Council, I might add. There is nothing left to chance, although I must admit there are some unexpected surprises along the way. Now did I answer your question?

David...I am sure we could go on with this conversation indefinitely; perhaps it is better off left to one of your future books when, *I am just guessing,* you have every intention of reintroducing this topic.

God...The nice thing about Soul memories is that once you have **seen the movie** of your life you do retain tidbits of information pertaining to future events. You David, are picking up on one those kernels now. In the continuum I see, *I know,* that My books have already been written, you just haven't typed them up for Me yet. But you will; it IS a crucial aspect of both yours and Celestial's personal and planetary destinies.

David...Yes, I know I have seen the movie, after all I wrote the script. Although I must admit it would be interesting to know **now** why I added certain shall I say, less desirable scenes in. All things in good time, right? Question, I am sure there are others beside ourselves who go to bed at night and wake up more exhausted than when we first went to bed. Any thoughts on this?

God...Thoughts no, an inner knowing, yes. David, I know that you know the reason behind this and yes, this is a good time to discuss this topic. All of you live two lives, one during the day when you are awake and the other while you sleep. Dependent upon who you are and your current evolutionary level, your *after hours* activities can sometimes be more intense than your wakened moments. It is during your sleep cycle that you reunite with others from your Soul Clusters to replenish, to analyze and then strategize on what best to do next. You have partial recall of some of these events when you awaken and remember your dreams. It also during these **down times** that many of you work both off and on world with other Star Keepers. The specific purposes behind these encounters is as varied as each of you is. Suffice it to say that in many cases you are better off not knowing, for it may distract you during the present, which is where your focus needs to remain.

As for the *less than desirable scenes,* let Me just say this and this pertains to everyone, there are karmic experiences each of you agreed to ahead of time in order to learn from the experiences. It matters naught if it was for personal reasons, or if you were involved simply for the purpose of providing another person with an experience they were in need of having. If you look back at those experiences you will find they had specific reasons for their having existed. What you glean from these is up to you. They are however the catalyst that helped to shape you into the person you are today. There will be plenty of time after you've moved on from this existence to look back upon them. For now, keep shifting your eyes to the horizon while having your feet firmly planted in the present.

David...I find it interesting that you chose in the title of this chapter to say "Brushes of Life" instead of "Brushes with Life." I have not read Celest's part yet, perhaps you have already addressed this.

God...Yes, I did and no, I did not. It all depends on how proficient one is at understanding My speaking in <u>God Code</u> (from the previous book *"Beyond the Veil ~ Epiphanies from God,"* i.e. reading between the lines.) Brushes with life could possibly refer to a form of first contact, something new that makes one realize that life is real and not a dream. Brushes of life is the artistic side of each of you where you as the artist is being an active participant in the Creation of your own personal world. As always there is more which could be shared, in My pursuit to continue being a good teacher I shall stop now by saying that I am simply speaking in "Godeneese," and that is My Choice.

God Talk 7

The History of the Chrysalis of the Individual Soul

God *(received by David)* The Souls of this world who initially arrived here faced many challenges that would not and could not be relevant to Souls living on other orbs, other realms. The evolutionary process is precise in its fervent choice to further advance the evolvement of the Eternal Soul. Soul instinctively knows that the only way to return to Source is to achieve balance and harmony on all levels of Its journey. Soul is by no means in a hurry to further enhance through achievement Its immortal status, nor should It be. *Why would It try to further enhance something that it already has,* you may ask. The ultimate quest for reunification with The Creator is not the end-all of a Soul's journey, Soul knows that when that time eventually comes it will be but another *of many* new beginnings. Literally Children, the stages and levels of the Chrysalis development never cease. This is another part of the Chrysalis of the individual Soul. This is how **history** is made.

There is something I want to speak of now that does indeed impact on the Chrysalis state as a whole. The search for the proverbial fountain of youth, for illusionary ideas of immortality, is causing a great many goodhearted Souls to lose their way. How can I best encourage each of you to just live your life and stop worrying about the inevitable process of dying? If you were to truly believe in reincarnation, only then would you understand that there is no need for you to try to accomplish everything in one lifetime. Would this not free you from your worries and concerns about acquiring enough to carry you through? Would you then allow yourself to **get a life** rather than trying to support and defend the one you are trying so desperately to hold on to?

Think of the infinite life patterns and instincts of plants. The plant species in its own form of wisdom, acknowledges that in every beginning there must be an end to the cycle. Cycles are formed to bring closure to a chapter which has ultimately run its course. Each course is set by the entity which initiated the cycle to begin with. As such, each climaxed occasion is just another step in the evolutionary process. I spoke earlier of the need for Souls in their individual clusters to try out new ideas and then share them with others. This is only the beginning. As I have so duly noted, We have given you the implements necessary for you to continue the evolutionary process. One being of course...reincarnation, two is the Creation of Soul clusters where the ongoing sharing process continues.

Three, is the Universal pool of knowledge and the Akashic Library where you may study, research and assimilate as much knowledge as is necessary to achieve your specific set of goals. These are but a few steps taken throughout your own individual chrysalis movement. There are limitless ways for you to acquire the tools necessary to start a brand new cycle and then successfully navigate your way through it and ultimately bring it to a satisfactory conclusion. Sounds like a piece of cake does it not? Well it is, IF, you do not get in your own way, which happens more often than not here on the Earth Star planet.

The maturation cycle of any Soul is dependent upon the will and the desire of the many *individual Selves* that Soul Creates <u>for</u> Itself along the way. Every aspect of Soul that have been uniquely separate entities at one time or another, contribute to the whole. In any given moment, Soul may have upwards to thirty or forty other forms of Itself, living out lives in different areas of this Universe and other Universes. Soul is not bound by limitations; however Its personas are. The limitations imposed are determined by the Over Soul. Each independent aspect of Soul utilizes the accrued knowledge it has gathered throughout its many incarnations, Its many Chrysalis cycles. This is one reason why some people on this world are more mature than others are. Maturity does not come with physical age; although it is true it manifests itself through experience and some people here do equate that with age. "Experiencing," is a major key to evolvement, so if you do not try anything new then there is no way to really understand it and then decide if that is what you may want to continue to do.

My dear ones, if I could just get you to take note for but a moment, of how blessed you are in all ways. You have been given a great opportunity here to be on the frontlines while actively participating in a very crucial timeline in human evolution. What you do with this Divine gift is up to you. I would however suggest that all those who are willing should take advantage of it, for it will not come again. This too is yet another stage of your individual development. I do not believe Terra would ever choose to repeat *any* of her prior experiences, the ones that had occurred with all the previous "yous." There is so much that each must experience in any given lifetime. From the mundane to the complex, each aspect must be dealt with through due diligence and right action. Do yourself a favor this time around and trim off some of the less fruitful, frivolous endeavors. You are making **history** here, do it with pride and honor. Concentrate on what is important; focusing on your Spiritual growth should be priority number one. This is the foundation that will support the groundwork for everything else that is to come later. Turn on the Light in your mind's eye, learn to SEE clearly. Learn to tune out all the extraneous noise and distortion. Keep your focus and be attentive, this is *not* the time to be lollygagging about.

I bring this up now because history, especially humanity's history, has a devious way of repeating itself. This simply will not do anymore, not if *you* are going to see your way through to the finish line. I ask you, how can any of you be satisfied knowing you could have done more to be of service to others and instead of doing so, you chose repetition and self-gratification as your life's pursuit? If Soul is to evolve it must be YOU contributing the best you have to offer every "thought" of the way. Each small step forward, whether it is through random acts of kindness, or through higher pursuits of much larger endeavors, does not matter. All I ask, all Soul asks, is that you do your best at all times.

Not many of you will ever know exactly what it is that you came here to do, you are not intended to know. That part of your Chrysalis history will be readily available after your *departure* from Earth. You will get glimmers along the way and for most of you, that will be enough. David was pondering on the idea the other day of how to be a bell ringer without actually sounding an alarm bell. Personally, I think both he and Celest are doing a marvelous job, their biggest question to themselves is, *"are we doing enough?"* I can assure you they are. The Paul Reveres of this world sound the alarm when danger is knocking on their doors, I am doing the same. The wisdom I am sharing with each of you at this time should have been common knowledge by now, but it isn't. The truths I wish to share with you are to aid and assist you while there is still time to do something beneficial with the information I am giving you. David, and others like him, are not sounding warning bells, although perhaps they should be. They understand and respect the Universal Laws pertaining to non-interference, so they instead choose to promote teaching relative to taking personal responsibility for your actions and non-actions.

Perhaps these sessions of Mine will not reach everyone in this current timeline, they will however be around for reference long after all of you have transitioned off this world once again. I have tried to impress upon you before that the dress rehearsal of life is over. Either you have it figured out for yourself by now, or you won't quite get it this time around. Because your school is out and as any good parent should do, I am asking you to step out into the world and fend for yourself with the tools you have on hand. If you weren't paying attention in class, then that is your loss. The Souls who graduate from the Earth Star Walk this time around will have earned their laurels; they will have satisfactorily <u>proven to themselves</u> all *they* needed to. They have written their <u>history</u> and will continue to do so.

Your history books are full of references of events which occurred and ultimately denoted specific alterations in your development as a civilization. The same goes for a Soul's evolution. Like each of you, an individual's growth process cannot be determined by any other than the individual himself. Either you want it or you don't. The question is, ***how badly do you want it***? Are you willing to give up everything else in order to attain a higher level of sentience? Can you willingly let go of *everything* in order to receive *everything* in return? Are you willing to go the extra mile when you are tired, worn-out and ready to give in? I watch these two scribes day in and day out, trying so valiantly to make a difference in others' lives. Therefore I will use them as examples. I am allowed to do that you know! They live without a safety net; they wouldn't know what to do with one if they had it. Day to day they never know what is coming next for them and yet day in and day out, they tirelessly do My work because that IS who they are. They ask nothing in return, yet they know full well that I will provide them all that they need. They keep their lives simple, yet their lives are as complex as can be. There is much that they would like to do and places they would like to see, yet they know that in these turbulent times, now is not the best time to do so. They heed Our sage advice. Our familiar voices are always in their heads cheering them on and comforting them when they are feeling a bit down. This is how it was always intended to be and yes, in most places in My Universe, this is exactly how it is. Celest and David don't stop to think about the evolution of their Souls, but you couldn't slow them down if you tried.

There is no linear equation that can accurately compute just how long it will take for any Soul to make Its journey through any level or any stage of the chrysalis process. Since time has no meaning, it would also make sense that nothing pertaining to an evolutionary scale can be set into a timeline situation. There are many variables to be considered; many *possibilities and probabilities* that must occur. Each Soul walks through their journey; some taking what you may term "centuries" to learn to just simply Be. There is no pressure, why should there be? There is an eternity available which the Chrysalis of the individual Soul may require in order to make Its journey to the top of the ladder. You see, what linear time has taught each of you is that there are false limitations imposed on just how long something should or must take to accomplish a task. This is only true on Earth; everything else in the continuum happens simultaneously, therefore there are no *time* restrictions. My suggestion to each of you is to understand that you only have so long to complete your chosen tasks here on Earth, before your physical time will obviously come to an end. Then you can once again pick up your Chrysalis self and continue your adventure, but at a different time. Acknowledge to yourself that **you can only do what you can do** and be satisfied with knowing that. Then set that thought aside and set your sight on manifesting the whole conceptualized sequence of living in a Chrysalis state at different points in your evolution. Of course you should leave out "the expectations" from the equation. There is no point in setting yourself up for disappointment, be proud of what you have accomplished and move on. You will move as far forward during any lifetime as you are capable of. In most cases you will find you have very little time left now, in comparison with what you will have available to you, once you have fully integrated with the ascension process and begun your first steps into living, existing, in the NOW-less time of the 4th and 5th dimensions. This is where Earth is heading. She will enter many more higher dimensions than you realize. A word of caution, if you find it difficult to accept living in the Now, here in the present, then you may have more work to do on preparing yourself to do so.

The different aspects of the chrysalis process have a resemblance to the chrysanthemums in your flower gardens. As varied as each is, each in every moment is in a different state of growth. Each chooses to utilize different gene configurations. Some are designed to make stems taller, the petals brighter and ultimately determine which color would best express its unique qualities. Once fully grown the flower itself determines how long it will remain in that state of being. Once it has completed its cycle it either goes into a dormant state awaiting the beginning of the next cycle, or it transitions to a higher plane of existence. Nothing is lost or destroyed; all matter is absorbed and reused.

However in your case, it is the essence of your Soul that retains the memories of each lifetime encounter, each vestige of information It has gathered and then adds it to the collective, which is the Higher you. Patience must always be exercised in the growth process, yet at the same time one who is living a physical experience must not take too long to *choose* to move onwards and upwards. No, this is not a contradiction in terms. If you choose to remain in a dormant state on a Spiritual level, or continually exist in a state of indecision or procrastination, the body will read these signs *as a choice made by the host*. This will be interpreted as a statement that it has no desires, ambitions, or purpose. This is when the body will start to rebel and begin showing signs of sickness from its "disease through disposition." Soul is finicky that way. It desires for Itself limitless expansion and to constantly flourish. It **will** let you know when It is dissatisfied with your personal progress.

I would like to take a moment and describe to you a small part of the relationship between the Soul and whatever Universe Soul resides in. This is **also** a part of the Chrysalis movement. Because everything is connected in ways that are generally unfathomable by someone who is having a physical experience, some of you may only be beginning to grasp what I am sharing here with you. The Chrysalis of the Soul deeply impacts upon this Universe and all Universes. As Soul expands Itself through choices made, so does the Universe that Soul is living in expand. Just as the **consciousness** of a **race** of beings expands it subsequently alters the frequency of vibration and the shape and scope of the sphere they inhabit. As this occurs the planetary consciousness is raised and consequently what was at one time considered to be *acceptable,* changes and it becomes quite apparent that the planetary consciousness is shape-shifting into a new configuration and a new paradigm of itself. I am speaking of what lies just beyond the field of vision of those people who only utilize their main senses. The people who reach beyond this point, those that accept that there are no limitations, are privy to sights and sounds which are normally considered to be outside of the physical realm. This is where you will see what goes on behind the scenes, such as the orbs which are showing up on your digital cameras. Other events include the conscious observation of the merging of dimensions which will manifest as dimensional doorways. If you wish to be excited about something that will never cease to amaze you, then I encourage you to seek out these new experiences.

I will leave you now with one further thought, the time you have left is not of importance, what IS important *is what you do with the allotted time you have.* You will never be able to turn back the hands of time to alter an experience for I will not allow it.

David...Thanks God, as always it was a pleasure being in your company.

God...You are welcome...Let's move on now shall We?

God (*received by Celest*) Among some of My more notable efforts during this period of re-education that I am sharing with each of you in order to further your conscious understanding of yourself, is this introduction to the state of yourselves in earlier times that are impacting upon each of you yet today. The today of your today is the precursor of all your tomorrows, remember? So it is that the yesteryear time periods set into motion the foundation that you have today, that you have as individual Souls walking in human form. It was during your early formative states that you each gathered either progressive inspirations that would define you as the truly awesome beings you truly are, or you gathered more **recessive** thoughts and lower-grade inspirations that you chose to be your "guiding Lights." During this period you all have the opportunity to alter your developing philosophies many times. These were not random acts; they were simply a type of swapping of ideals and ideas from one dimensional realm to the others. It was in this manner that you each were able to share wondrous ideas with others in your Soul Cluster who shared some of the ideals you were Creating for yourselves.

You see there was no time limit imposed upon any of you. This is a Sacred process, this bringing into the matrix of your Soul your upcoming lifetimes and experiences. This is but part of the reason why so many, many, of you have returned again and again to previously held convictions. None of you attempted to beguile the others; your innocence and pureness of thought and Spirit were easily seen by each of Us, We who are the Luminescents as well as by all those others who surrounded you and watched over you. You each knew that service to others must never be compromised by service to self. These were long periods of conviviality that were shared not exclusively with you; they were shared with all Souls at the gathering. Ah, the wonderment of those times never ceases to delight Me! So much positive and beauteous possibilities and probabilities were explored by you each. You each also understood the portent of future events on the Earth Star planet and on other planets and defined them to yourselves as "things to come." You were very much aware of the significance all these future possible and probable events would have for all of you as individuals and the impact they could have on your individual Soul Clusters. Because none of you at that time were wearing human form, none of you were intractable in your thought patterns.

Because free expression is vital for each Soul that has ever been Created to possess and to enhance to the best of their own ability, no restrictions, no limitations are ever placed upon any of you during this development state. You each freely asked all of Us questions about anything you either did not understand, or about the things you did understand **on one level,** the Super Conscious level, but experienced difficulty understanding as you viewed the slow development process that was taking place in the human race. None of you were overcome by the egregious and outrageous thoughts the people on Earth were emitting. None of you found fault with the Children on Earth who were committing atrocities against one another. Instead, your innate compassion found a home, a place to send your compassion to. So you all generously sent it to Earth. Of course you did not form any judgment calls, you did not know how to and did not agree with that thought pattern anyway!

One of the most common forms of what you considered to be irrational behavior on the part of the human race was that so many of those Children were absolutely implacable in their own determination of how things should be and how to keep other people enslaved to illusions. No, none of this was a judgment on others; you simply stated it as you felt it to be. I want you all to understand please, that the type of innocence you all share during the chrysalis periods is a pureness and openness and an unlimited ability to be receptive to all the Greater Truths and Realities. Constraint does not exist during those periods, although oftentimes your Guardians had to work very diligently to convince you to slow down a bit and not to try to assimilate all the information too quickly. The irony here is that then you needed to be slowed down and now you need to speed up!

The grand diversity that exists between each of the Soul Clusters yet is <u>shared</u> by each is something that is a fine example of both the tangible and the intangible working in tandem. As you each progressed to higher more evolved stages of learning and understanding there, you each made decisions that would prove to be relevant to your future incarnations, regardless of whatever planet you chose to inhabit, or We, who are the Luminescents, chose for you. I can not say an actual grading process takes place there; rather it is a Spiritual type of gradient that shows you each very clearly how much more you may want to learn and how much progress your developmental state is affecting your individual Soul Clusters. Ok, for every epoch of development there exists an equal opposite of non-development. So it is that when a Soul intentionally arrives at a crux of an important matter, usually this occurs when Soul is deciding how vulnerable It really wants to be after the incarnation process has occurred, it is then that certain decisions are made by those Souls. These are the decisions that will clearly define what type of life experience, the duration of such and if and when a Soul chooses to cross the line for the **experience** of living a life of debauchery, rather than a life of evolvement, is arrived at. Although this may sound confusing to some of you, choosing a life of immoral behavior may actually be a step in the direction of evolution if the Soul tires of that experience quickly and does not choose to repeat it. It is here in this realm, when Souls attain that certain gradient alignment that is so necessary, so vitally important to Each of them as well as to their own Soul Clusters, that certain levels of Soul maturity are in a sense "categorized" and aligned with other Souls whose maturity AT THAT TIME, along with their own desires, intents and self-chosen lessons and finales in a lifetime, are placed together in a group. Thus clusters of Souls will in effect enter a life experience with only their sentience to be their conscious guide....IF they had included that factor to be part of their off-world experience. These clusters will be accompanied in a manner of speaking, by the other individual Souls from their own Soul Cluster and oftentimes many, many, Souls from other Soul Clusters who have also agreed to participate in the others' life experiences, in one manner or another.

Although I can not say that I like the term "categorize" when I am speaking of these Sacred formations of the beings of Light, I do know of the necessity of being as clear with you each as non-humanly possible. Soul formations are a tremendous amassing of the luminous nature of MySelf, all other Luminescents, the Creator, the Creation processing and all other parts of Divinity. As these diverse formations of Souls who have joined forces for the purpose of propagating the Light of Gods and Goddesses here on the Earth Star as well as in other worlds and other Universes, gather together and exchange holy communion through the telepathic ability they all have, an almost indefinable sense of great peace and expectancy descends upon these groups. I have stated before that Light begets Light; so it is that a cohesiveness of Light Matter exists among Us all that is made manifest within the very core of each Soul. Before these Souls are placed into their designated groups, they first must clearly understand what their Soul status is *at that moment.* It is because of that necessity, the very realistic need to understand and be in awareness of their status that Souls then have the privilege of conjoining with other specific Soul groups.

There are the Souls who have decided that they may only desire to have a tiny taste of life here on the Earth Star, for instance. These ones have already predestined their own early departure from mortal form. IF however, during their incarnation here any of these Souls decide that perhaps they may want to stay longer, then they MAY add an addendum to their Soul Contact, their own Soul Agreement. IF this happens then yes, others who are part of that group of "Souls in agreement" MAY also have the choice of remaining longer, if that is what they truly want.

No decision is made haphazardly. Many matters must be taken into careful consideration since obviously the wrong decision made for the wrong reason would be sure to wreak havoc upon those Souls.

Another grouping of Souls would have banded together whose primary interests would be in the scientific or medical fields. These ones usually choose a longer period of a life experience because they are already aware that because of their selected fields, they will need all the time they can have in order to attempt to implement good changes within those areas. Obviously after they arrive here and attain a chronological age when they can work in their self-destined professions, many of these Souls become discouraged. They find that regardless of how hard they work to disassociate themselves from the illusions of truth that are so rampant in those professions, they feel they are at the mercy of a non-fecund force. They are correct. However before their descent here they were aware of the tremendous odds they faced, yet the majority of them were confident that if they tried hard enough, they could help change the ways of this world.

Another formation would be those who have been attracted to the world of politics. It is not long after they become involved in the political arena that they soon discover to their chagrin that their true enemy that they must try to destroy is the secret governments behind the governments. Ostensibly the KNOWN governments appear to work in effecting good change for the Earthizens on this planet, however more and more the Souls in politics are discovering that they are really in deep battle against the **shadows.** These normally hardy Souls not only become disillusioned quickly, there is a great tendency for so many of them to lose themselves to drugs.....and worse.

Many, many, more Souls than you realize choose a life of penury not only for the learning experience it offers, but also to reestablish themselves as Children of this planet who can and do learn to live in a more simple fashion, thereby negating any thought they may have had of malice of forethought directed against those other Children who possess so much more. Perhaps you should all remember that the next time you encounter homeless people. You never know who you are really speaking with.

Of course Souls who chose to be of the religious persuasion do not always intend that it be a lifelong experience. However, the tentacles of religions, just as those of politics, can have long reaching repercussions targeting those who have "left the fold."

Souls who have chosen wealth and power may be ones who have at one time or another been part of a formation that abused wealth and power and are returning as a personal test to see if they can and will change their prior behavior and actually help other less fortunate people. Well, all I can say about that is ...you can see how well that is going. "The truest test of a human being is how they handle power." Although that is actually Blue Star the Pleiadian's quote, I feel it is important to repeat it here in order to make My point.

Now of course I will move on to another massive formation that too is comprised of Souls from all other Soul Clusters. These are the Spiritual Warriors, both walk-ins and born-ins alike. I can not give any of you exact numbers on any of these Soul formations for they are always changing. They try to learn to walk in one another's shoes, so to speak. However, these Warriors who are teachers and healers as well, have from the first nano-moment that they decided exactly what they wanted to do in order to serve as procreators, as vectors in a sense, nearly always return again and again in order to further combat evil and change what they can. They do so while not breaking any Universal Laws while they are on their quest to defeat the purveyors of deceit. I will not at this time speak of the walk-ins who are an important part of this formation. I will speak of them later in this book however.

Spiritual Warriors are those who have throughout the process of incarnating many, many, times made a Sacred vow to themselves on an individual basis that is, that clearly delineates how they best feel they can serve the Universe at any given time. It is sad in a manner of speaking, that there is a necessity for Souls to choose this role. Yet without them, many worlds could easily have been lost, defeated during the spatial timelessness that exists everywhere. The Warriors in this formation know one another very well, even though there are always incoming, "newbies" who have not yet learned enough in order to be placed on the front line. The mission of those who are of this formation is simple yet complex at the same time. They are to teach, teach, teach, while engaging in non-physical combat when it is necessary to protect and defend other Children here on this planet. Those people whose missions are to alter the world of politics, medicine, Spirituality, technology and others are much needed to ride the NESARA Winds. Although I stated that it should be non-physical combat, over the centuries here clusters of Souls have also had to engage in physical combat just to protect their own lives and to protect those other Souls walking in human form that can not yet protect themselves. I am not going to get technical here in this book, at least I will try not to, so I will not explore the various ways these Warriors use pure energy and fashion it into a weapon that can and will defeat those who are the attacking predators.

Soul formations that chose parenting for their own personal reasons have a path as fraught with anxiety as do the other formations. Bringing babies into this world and trying to instill morals that may only be relative to the parents themselves, usually becomes a tug-of-war situation as the young child grows up. Parenting is a test of fortitude for many, this is true, however there are many lessons that Souls learn about themselves as well as about others through this process. This is not a life choice to be taken lightly.

I am hoping that by My explaining these formations to you, you will better understand, or perhaps begin to understand, your own self and the role you have been enacting and why. I also told you that sentience is the only energy you have when you enter the physical life. It is not that you do not have other gifts and abilities; it is that sentience is Soul and MySelf speaking to you and through you at any moment. It is this, but it is also more than this. I did tell you that if sentience has been chosen by you as a trusted aid and perhaps considered to be of vital importance, then you can succeed beyond your own expectations if you use it. Yes, there are people who bring their sentience with them but "lose" it while here. The reasons are many; some because their minds become too overwrought to focus on this ability; others have minds and hearts that become hardened by life experiences. They have become jaded. These are just a couple of reasons why. Obviously whatever conditioning a person is exposed to here will also diminish sentience. Some Souls, not many, choose not to enter here with all their sentience intact. It is not really that they are looking at human life as the challenge it truly is, it is more that they have decided to test their own mettle to see how well they can do. Personally, I would advise you to never leave home without it!

The people who have lived their lives here whether the experience was one of longevity or not, always touch others' lives for better or for worse. While on Earth however, there is no person who can in any way accurately quantify precisely how much good he or she has been able to accomplish here. Although they have spent so much time working with others through teaching sessions and feel that the others may have actually learned all that was being taught to them, it must be remembered that *people change.* You may have worked and worked and worked through parenting, medicine, and politics or as a Warrior, until you believed that you gave as much as you could and still see no results among the others. This is when things can become to feel as though you, yourself, have failed. It is a desultory feeling to be sure, but one that is totally erroneous. Dear Souls, how many times have I and others told you each and all that you can only do what you can only do. Far too many of you are just too hard on yourselves. This happens because of your fervent desire to not only be all you can be, but to <u>instill</u> that virtue in others as well. As long as you are being all you are capable of being, the rest will take care of itself.

You are not in any manner responsible for how others think or what they do, as long as you, yourself, are only working towards the greater good. You are not responsible for making the others, *"slaves in training."* Those people who are the main contributing force to moral decay always find the victims they seek. The people who are themselves still enslaved to depraved indifference and have lost their own humanity will see the Light at a future time. Either way, that is not your problem. I agree however that there are times when a person who has muffled Soul Voice almost to the point of extinction, may find that it is very possible to have a confrontation *with one's self* and still lose the battle. You may mull this statement over until such time that you understand it. Moral turpitude is not a pretty sight; so it is that when Souls leave the Earth Star planet for example and return to Nirvana, they all have the opportunity to rechrysalis as a means for gathering more pure knowledge based on their previous life experience and on the life experiences of other people they encountered. Hmm, My Celest-Self is having a bit of anxiety because of My choice of the word, "rechrysalis." She is repeatedly telling Me that no such word exists that she knows of in the human language. However, since I decided that this is My word of choice, I shall use it anyway.

Souls may return again and again to the unique cocoon that shields them from mistruth and protects them while they are in the resting state, or the "understanding" state, reviewing plans and ideals that had gone awry. Regardless of all they had undergone they have still contributed to the unlimited expansion of the life force of their individual Soul Cluster and of course of the main OverSoul Cluster as well.

Celest...God, during the early formative times, the stages of early growth, how do Souls interact with the more mature Souls who are returning to Nirvana? Is there any integration there among them and do they decide that they may want to participate with one another in a future time?

God...The returning Souls always require long periods of rest and need to be replenished because of all they had endured in the recently departed mortal life. It is imperative that they each receive this. All Souls in Nirvana are highly respectful of those requirements. The returning

Souls themselves decide when, not *if*, they are ready to be receptive to the early growth Souls. Yes, Celest, as this occurs there is a symbiotic relationship between them. You see, readers, each of the returning Souls has already had so many, many, experiences that the younger ones have not yet had. Because they have had them, they are in the unique position of offering sage advice to those who will be departing. Many *future* agreements take form there; this is when the Souls know who they want to collaborate with at a different time, in a different place.

All Souls have the ability to learn from one another's experiences. All Souls are receptive and most willing to assist all other Souls about life on other worlds, especially life on the Earth Star. The Universal Law of "Action and Reaction" is clearly seen in this realm. This means that all Souls do have the ability and the empathy to commiserate with one another about prior errors in judgment that may have occurred during any life walk. Many visions take place here; visions Created by the Collective Souls. It is in this manner that a Soul can and does assist in Creating wondrous ideas and better understanding of the necessity of having morals. This is all I will say about this at this time. Ok?

Celest...Thank you God, and yes of course it is "ok."

God Talk 8

The Gone but not Forgotten

God *(received by Celest)* Children, I want you to consider the serious implications of what I am about to tell you. In mortality, you all observe people who die physical deaths. Some people really have no interest about the death of a specific individual if the person who has passed over was not someone they really cared for or about anyway. Some people enter into a grieving process that may last throughout their own mortality. Someone somewhere coined the phrase, "the good die young." First of all I do not agree with that in the least. However, it seems to be some type of soothing mental and emotional balm for many people. Of all the fears I have seen Created here on the Earth Star planet, the one I consider to be the most heinous is your fear of physical death. Children, life is not a "shell game." I have gone to great lengths to impress upon each of you the value and importance of mortal life. Do any of you truly believe that I would agree to act as co-creator of the human race and be in agreement that all people, all life forms, would have the opportunity to rebirth over and over and over again, if life did not have value? All right then, in order to rebirth you must die a physical death. It is this simple, is it not?

Many of you have undergone certain experiences on Earth that have either caused you to have a deep-seated fear of death or to have an equally deep-seated fear of life. For millions of people everywhere, both fear of death and fear of life exist in equal proportions. I do know of course how religions have parlayed that fear of death and the nonsense belief that reincarnation does not exist, into an equal opportunity to have you each be dependent upon the religion you were either born into or chose for yourself. You see, people who have come to rely on their religious icons and religious teachers to decide for **them** what is real and what is not, are today Spiritual eunuchs. Now that you know the human race has been castrated, how do you feel about it and what do you want to do in order to change it?

Mortality = mortal. Yes, you are mortal, that is a necessity. In order to rise to new, higher levels of your Golden Self you must first build the foundation that allows you to ascend from one level, one form, to another. Is this really so difficult for you Children of the Earth to understand? You know that I and the other Luminescents are immortal. In time you will each understand the stupendous effort that had to be undertaken in order for all life species to possess the necessary elements, the important catalysts required to breathe breath into the physical form. You were designed to first live many lives of mortal nature. This is also the way of life of the ancient civilizations on other worlds and in other Universes. Although their life spans are much longer than yours are today, they too have had their growing pains amid a *type* of physical pains as well. Perhaps I should have suggested that human Children, all Earthizens everywhere, should have been required to take a course in "Life 101" followed by "Death 102." However, that would have cut short your own innate abilities to listen to your own hearts, minds and Spirits. As a teacher, I too must know when to assign homework to the students and when to retreat and allow them to figure some things out for themselves. I do so out of the greatest respect for each of you. If you can understand that life is not truly respected by all people here on this planet, then maybe... just maybe, you can understand that death is not either. Physical death has its own patina; its own adventure, its <u>understood</u> sentience of spatial gridline intersections. It is a tad ironic that there have been and still are millions of people here who daily pray for their own deaths in order to free themselves from something or other. While they are busily praying for death, they are not really living, now are they?

Guilt is a byproduct of insecurity about things that had not been understood or properly cared for. Yet in truth, guilt itself is a human-made commodity; Soul does not indulge in useless activities! It is when people pass over from mortal life that guilt seems to bind the main mourners to a senseless wringing of the mental faculties. People tend to think they should have acted or reacted differently to the feelings and thoughts of the person who had passed over while that individual was still in mortal form. Although that may have been the truth in many cases, IF My Children truly understood not only the importance of physical death but the equal importance of the mourners celebrating the passing over from one life in order to gain yet another, you would not all be in the mental shambles that you are today. Mortality can be difficult enough in most cases, so why work at making it even more so? So it is that while the recently departed are resting and regrouping in Nirvana, the friends and families on Earth feel a sense of loss. Some Children have been heard to think, "I feel that mom's death is a violation of my peace of mind." Well, perhaps these people should ask mom about that one.

There is no violation in this process. Some people love too well while others love too less. Of course there is a remarkable bond that exists in most cases, between the departing Soul and some of the surviving clan. However, what no one here wants to readily admit to themselves, let alone speak of publicly, is that when someone who has been close to you, or you have good affection for has passed over, **it reminds you of your own mortality.** Children, to not believe in the reincarnational process is to not believe in yourself. If you do not believe in yourself then you can not trust yourself or others. People who feel cheated when a loved one has departed fail to truly understand that there is no cheating involved. You each have your own gridline intersections to meet and I really would prefer that you did so while on good terms with yourself. It is the memories that you shared, some of which you cherished, that remind you oh so painfully of what you think you have lost. Although you have not really lost anything, so many of you think there is a void that you believe is in your life as a result of another's physical death. "Grief" is a result of a misunderstanding of yourself and your emotions. People do not, well, stable people do not, grieve when a Child is born. It is in most cases a cause for celebration. How many of you have ever given the slightest thought to who or what that Child may have been **before** that recent reincarnation?

I encourage each of you to by all means keep your cherished memories of the loved one; but use those memories to further expand your own foundation in life. To further enhance your own life you can take the time to muse about what good actions you may be able to take in this life based upon some of the ideas and ideals of the one who has left. No, you will not be mimicking the other; it is a simple matter of sharing and co-joining with the other's good thought waves. It does not mean you must follow all of the departed's beliefs. As independent Spirits you have the right to keep or discard those beliefs you can not treasure or respect in any way. No, that will not upset mom who is in NIRVAVA. She is already wiser than she was while in mortal form. Psychiatrists and psychologists take note please; We do not ever leave any Soul behind. Although We know exactly how they have lived their lives and what actions they have taken or failed to take, the memory signature of all they truly are remains with Us for eternity. Dealing with patients about issues of grief should always clearly delineate how much better off a survivor will be by the simple act of accepting what could not be changed and by honoring the life of the other person. Honoring is simple to do; it simply requires that people remember the good that was achieved and release any of the bad memories. The greatest honor any person can bestow upon the departed person is simply saying, "you did well," and then release yourself from the grip of grief. Obviously if you truly believe they did not do well, just say goodbye.

Yes, of course I know that millions of people did not do well with other people. I know far better than you do of the atrocities committed by so-called loving people against other people. That however does not mean that you should relish the fact that they are gone. If you do so you would be doing the wrong thing for the wrong reason. In all cases of physical death consider what lessons, what experiences you had with them that may have contributed to your growth. They are always there if you bother to look. Those who proclaim they never received any benefit from the experiences are deluding themselves, **because they have.** No Soul here or on the other realms and dimensions is ever forgotten. The very sentience of Soul to Soul contact alone makes that an impossibility. I do not love My Hitler son any less than I love My Dali Lama son. Obviously I know more about both of them than do you. I do not love you, yourself, less than I love another, although I may have loved others longer. Ok, let us see if you understand that statement.

Millions and millions of My Earthbound Children have lost their lives during cataclysmic events. Many more still will. As this has happened and will continue to do so, grief is accompanied by utter shock. This should not be so, for after all you do not know of their pre-birth agreements or of the designated timelines. Again, it is your own mortality factor that is scaring you. As long as you have the fears about death, as long as you refuse to just accept the inevitability of leaving mortal flesh sans regrets, then you are truly harming yourself. I have heard people say that they only fear what they can not see; but in truth they fear the unknown. Because there is so much controversy about reincarnation and the "afterlife," it is somewhat understandable that the human race would not be feeling too amiable about the thought of passing over into *"the unknown."* Children, death is not your enemy; ignorance is. I have stated in one of My previous books that I do not know the exact moment any of you will leave your mortality. I simply await your arrivals. How anyone chooses to leave the mortal life is contingent upon many factors and events occurring on the planet. I do know however that if you live with great integrity and honor, then shall you pass over with these qualities intact. Those whose lives have been rife with tension and unhappiness will still leave with a type of relief or acceptance. To die ignobly is also a choice. When all is said and done it is all up to you.

Celest...God, I appreciate how beautifully, how tactfully, you handled this sensitive subject. I am tying to think of the best way to phrase a question that I believe will be on the minds of many people. God, how relative to the subject of physical death is an individual's sentience when the subject is **that** person's impending passing over and how does sentience itself play into that final curtain of a life experience?

God...Whew Celest, that is a series of questions within questions! However, yes, I too feel that these are important questions. Sentience is an all-knowing energy in the sense that it has the ability to fully incorporate with all the feelings, emotions and love or hate based issues each person has. It also works with Soul Voice if the person in question is following the path of truth, honor and justice. Sentience is always in a state of awareness of itself. Sentience can and WILL impact on an individual's decisions or choices that need to be made. However if the person's mind and Spirit are filled to the brim with dross, sentience can not be of much assistance. Bearing this in mind, yes, sentience is in a state of awareness of when a person's time period either has arrived or will be arriving shortly, that will culminate in the passing over from mortal life. Once again I tell you that sentience is aligned with Soul Voice. The **conscious** energy of any mortal MAY work in conjunction with Soul Voice WHEN and IF certain conditions are met. The state of awareness that is actually sentience in activated motion exists on whatever level the person themselves is on. This in no way means that only the physical sensations are a result of the awareness (sentience) movement. There are people who do only act or react to physical stimuli. This can be considered to be a form of sentience.

However, true sentience is the activated awareness of all levels of understanding *non-logically,* situations, events, circumstances and so forth, thereby raising the level of evolutionary status for the people who have THIS gradient quality. I use the term "gradient" because it is a necessary part of the learning arc that all people must experience. Although you are all sentient beings, not all of you use or even know you have any level of awareness. The most evolved people on this planet use their sentience in concert with their lives. These people combine the *Super Conscious* knowing with the *conscious* parts of themselves. They may do so in an *unconscious* manner part of the time, but it works well for them regardless.

Because of the harmonious relationship between Soul Voice and sentience, the "awareness" energy gleans from Soul Voice the information relative to when the time for the human to depart has arrived or shall arrive posthaste. Oftentimes as this occurs sentience will nudge the person to make contact with certain people or to tie-up loose ends and at times can soothe the upcoming path by offering comforting thoughts and loving endearments. I understand why you used the term, "final curtain" Celest, however because Soul and sentience know that it is merely an "intermission," they simply try to be the staunch reassuring energies that they are. I believe this information should suffice.

Celest...Thank you God, I would say that it does.

God (received by David) Let Me begin by reminding each of you of the agreements made by you before entering into the Earth Star plane. These agreements you made centered on what was deemed to be of importance to you during this incarnation. Since all of you have been on the Earth Star Walk many times before, let Me remind each of you that you have all lost someone who was close to you and despite that loss... life did go on. Honor the memories of those who have gone before you by drawing from their strengths and learning from their weaknesses. Cherish the memories, but let go of the past. The dearly departed have left because it was their time to leave. It may not have been the timeline **you** may have wished for, so I ask you to remember, the choice was never yours to make.

Those of this world who may have been instrumental in bringing to light some of your greatest discoveries and achievements are never forgotten when they transition from this world. Some of you may forget who invented the telegraph wires, the internal combustion engine or the spinning wheel, but most of you will never forget the

George Washington apple tree story, or that it was the Wright brothers who flew the first plane. Each of you remembers parts and pieces of your history; typically you remember those which had an impact upon you personally, or those that society proclaims to be noteworthy. I would like to say to you, yes you, the one who is now reading My words, that **you** will be remembered for your actions and deeds, for your trials and tribulations as well as your successes and accomplishments. Your *Book of Life* is being written by your own hand and detailed records will be kept of all your sojourns. Every stop you've taken along the way, every thought you ever had, every dream you've ever dreamed, every ambition you have ever had, every kind or coarse word you ever uttered has been recorded. I feel some of you shuddering and perhaps you should. Others are nodding their heads in thoughtful remembrance of what they believed to be true. Even though many of you believed certain things to be true, very few of you ever stood up and mentioned those things out loud.

Those who came before you, those that were the risk takers and the truth talkers, will long be remembered for being perhaps not the first people of their kind, but for being able and willing to take a <u>Stand</u> for their beliefs, when there may have been an easier road to travel. Not everyone is meant to be a leader; however every one of you must at some point be willing to take a passionate position, your own declaration that clearly elucidates the meaning of "right can defeat might." This position is not merely about what you believe is correct. *You are making a statement of INTENT.* When this will occur is completely up to you. I just know that at some point it will happen, *hopefully*, much sooner than later.

There have been many animal and plant species that have come before you that some of you may consider now to be gone forever, if not forgotten. Each species has its own specific purpose for being, its own predetermined lifespan and its own desire to evolve into a finer, if not somewhat different version of itself. This is how it has always been; how it was intended to be. This is in great part the most important aspect of the Creative process. Each life form was Created carefully and imbued with the desire to reach beyond its original programming and as such, each must decide for itself when it is ready to take the next step and move up to the next evolutionary level. The choice is always their own, let Me be clear about this. The Universal Laws pertaining to non-interference always takes precedence.

Let us speak briefly about fact, fiction, myth, reality, even legend. If you scroll back through your history books, not the ones of today but the original documents which held more accurate interpretations of the *then* current events, you will begin to better understand how an innocent or intentional twist of a word here, an insertion of phrase or an incorrect personal interpretation there, can alter the true meaning of an event as the years pass. Some of you now refer to this as, *when fact becomes legend and legend inevitably becomes myth* or fiction. Children, let yourself not be fooled, the ghosts and goblins of yesteryear, the winged horse and the so-called monsters of the deep, were as real as you or I are and may be gone from your current reality but most certainly are not forgotten. Did you know that the legendary Loch Ness monster is not only real, but it has been on this world far longer than any of you could imagine. Many years past, back to the timeline you refer to as 2003, both Celest and David were fortunate enough to see one of these remarkable creatures. Were they in merry old Scotland or down in the Amazon? No, as a matter of fact they were in Washington State in the good old U.S.A. Now I ask you, what are the chances of them being in the right place at just the right time to see this, and who would believe them if they came forth and told their story? What they both know to be true is that these creatures have an extremely long incubation period and this is in small part why their numbers and subsequent sightings are so few.

I gather from your first impressions that you are on some level or another understanding what I am saying to each of you. Now what about those others whom you may consider to be lost to the history books? There have been so many good teachers who have walked this world and records of their journeys were never recorded here. I ask that you honor them as you would any of My Platos or Socrates. What about the inventor of string or the fork, knife and spoon for example, where would you be right now if they had not come along? What about the first person who learned how to swim? If they had not taught other people where would you all be now? That would have seriously limited your abilities to explore new continents, now wouldn't it? What about all those other unsung heroes that never get a mention? Do We not all owe them a debt of gratitude for their contributions to this world, no matter how small or seemingly insignificant their contributions were? The records of all these Souls' good deeds are archived in **THE LIBRARY** for all to see. They have not been forgotten.

Now what about all those that you may seriously wish to never have to think about again, those such as the Hitlers, Napoleons, Jack the Rippers and so on? Should they rightfully be long gone and forever forgotten? Tell Me, where would that leave you? Would you not feel cheated in knowing that the memories of them and all that they had done had been removed from existence? I ask you, what is it that YOU learned from them that no other person could have taught you?

Long forgotten are the Dudley DoRights and the Joan of Arcs of days gone past. Many of these were the teachers, the philanthropists, poets and healers of the time. On the flip side of the coin were the tyrants that plagued each of them. It was not always easy for any Soul to move forward in any lifetime with someone breathing down their necks, demanding they *cease and desist* or they would *cease to exist*. There were a great many goodhearted Souls that came before you who died such horrific deaths, all due to their desires to right the wrongs that were being imposed upon the human race. As those practitioners of the dark arts transitioned from this world their replacements were lying in wait, ready to enter this realm and they did not wait long to pick up where their predecessors had left off. Through the use of sword, spear and twisted tongue, the elite loudly proclaimed dominion over those too weak to stand in their way. Now those that **appeared** to have cheated another person out of a successful lifetime, more often than not, did just the opposite. You see, they knew little of the indomitable Human Spirit and its desire to survive. The harder they pushed, the more they took away, the stronger the peoples' desire to fight back became. What applied back then still applies today, the hungrier people become, the more they are taken for granted and their needs ignored, the louder their protests will become. No one likes to be considered expendable and rightly so. We who are the watchers kept a keen eye on those that had been abused and belittled. We noted their strengths and their weaknesses. We encouraged them to fortify their strong points, and then We taught them to play *their controllers'* game, against their controllers, only play it better. It was in this manner that the scales of justice began to slowly swing the other way. These Souls I am speaking of here now, are the same ones who have come back time after time to teach each succeeding generation of the need for positive change to enter into this world. These Souls may be long departed from the Earth Star but they are certainly not forgotten, especially when their legacies of promoting truth and justice is carried on through all of you.

What saddens Me is not just the abhorrent loss of life which occurred throughout your many relationships with this world, that was inevitable. What is sad is the loss of all those Sacred teachings that We all shared with the human race, that were intended to be passed down to each succeeding generation that was to follow. You see, there were GODLY amounts of knowledge passed on to the

Children of this world so that they would be better prepared, better able to cope with the realities of life in a physical world. In the beginning We taught you how to make fire, fortunately that information was not lost or many of you would have never survived a winter. We taught you to farm, to irrigate and be conservative in your needs, so there would always be plenty to go around. Well, you can see how well that went. Most people simply want more and more, and yes, this has upset the delicate balance of nature. We taught you the need to remember your origins, your purpose for being and to pass on these truths to your children's children. We taught you to use minerals and herbs to promote a healthy body; most of these teachings are no longer passed down. The minerals We showed you that were precious for their healing abilities were sadly converted to a form of monetary exchange. OK, what I am about to share with you **should have been common knowledge** by now; no longer can "you the stewards" continuously consume the resources of this world without consequences. No longer will it be allowed. You have been warned for the final time.

We are going to take a journey now, out beyond the realms of what is known as the physical realm. Here, where everything is happening simultaneously, there is a great calm in the air. There is no pressure, no anxiety, and no despair. There is no great impatience to get things right, because everything is known to be happening as it should. Most of you on the Earth Star plane are not privy to this *inner knowing*, for you closed that connection long ago. It is time to repair those severed connections so that you too, may once again join in and reinforce the life cord each of you possesses. It is this cord that ties you in with the collective Creative force. Once this has been accomplished none of you will ever again feel as if you are alone, you will never feel as if you have been forgotten about. Never was the human race abandoned; We have always been right here, where We said We would be. Here for each and every one of you. The isolation techniques introduced by those who have fallen from grace were very effective. With their introduction of religions, class distinction, the haves and have not's, a wedge was placed between all of you, thus dividing and segregating you. They effectively pitted you against each other and most of you were too blind to see this. <u>Spirituality, as I have said, unites people, religions divide them.</u>

Let Us take these diversionary tactics one step further. Imagine if you will for a moment what this world would have been like had there not been emperors and kings to rule over you. Imagine what it would be like not to have two vastly different versions of democracy trying to be imposed upon you. Imagine if you will that the time of the money lenders never began and that everyone just "had" everything they needed to survive. Imagine if you will a world where the air was clean, the soil fertile and the waters so pristine, you could almost feel the oxygen coursing through your veins as you immersed yourself in it. This is in small part the world that awaits you. It is not however here yet and therefore you must do what you can to bring all of this *and so much more* into manifested form. I know you are all suffering because of the abuse of this world's resources. I know that many of you are hungry, upset and so solitary. I promised you I would never leave you and *I have* kept that promise. If you will let Me, I will guide you to the place you need to be and show you the work that is still left undone. My other Children and I will teach you how to rekindle the Creative process in your hearts and minds. We will **remind** you of all that has been long forgotten. We will reunite you with your off-world families so that you may gain strength from this joining together. Then, just maybe, you will understand that even long after you leave this world a part of you will always be here with her. Your indelible Spirit cannot be crushed, it may be stifled from time to time, but it never dwindles and fades away. I am asking the seemingly impossible of all of you. I am asking you to believe, to have faith in your SELF.

No matter how many good works My Star Keeper Children perform, no matter how many messages those of the Spirit World send to those *whose ears are open*, no matter if you all grabbed a hold of the brass ring and won the lottery, the troubles of this world would not be over. None of you would have what you truly need until you first believe in yourself. Far too many of you have gone your separate ways and now you cannot find your way back home. It is you who have forgotten what was really important. We are going to rectify that, one Soul at a time if need be. It may not happen overnight, it may happen in a hundred years for some, but mind you... it will happen. Later on you will look back at all that you have endured and realize that as painful as it was, it was never as bad as it **could have** been. I have told you this before but it bears repeating: life has never been about the destination, it has always been about the journey. I bid you good day....for now.

David... What would you say to those who believe that "parents should never have to outlive their children?"

God... I would tell them what I always have, the choice was never theirs to make. It is not about *"we may not always understand God's will"* nor is it some form of punishment for *"sins committed by your forefathers."* Physical death comes to you all, when it happens is up to the individual, or circumstances beyond their control. As always I would encourage each grieving parent to celebrate the life now gone, not mourn it. You will be doing them a disservice if you continually mourn.

David... When families and friends grieve over the loss of a loved one, how does this impact upon the recently departed one?

God... David, since this one touches close to home I will share with the readers what I once asked you to share with your Earthbound relative who was personally going through this. The departed Soul, even though no longer in physical form, feels all the emotions you are going through, in many cases much more intensely than you may be. Some of these recently departed Souls cannot move on until this has been resolved. There is always an energetic residue that follows these type of unsettling thought patterns. So please, if you know someone, or if you personally are going through this grief process, thank the departed one for the time they had shared with you and let them go.

David... Thank you God, I believe that needed to be addressed.

God Talk 9

Intergalactic Relationships and the effect on Planet Earth

God *(received by Celest)* Well now, I hear the most titillating thoughts about how each of you define your origins and the dreams and sometimes fanciful ideas you have about where you are really from. In a sense I find it most understandable that Earthbound Children are finally questioning what they had at one time thought of as "preposterous." In another sense I understand far better than nearly all of you here why such intense longing descends upon you when you gaze at the stars and watch the ships flying overhead. These passionate feelings are natural occurrences for all those who have not fallen under the spell of ignorance. It is true however, that even many of the unilluminated Children do also from time to time, briefly wonder where they came from. Well, I can say with great authority I might add, that I know where you each came from but **not** where all of you will go. THAT is determined by your own hand. Each of you has arrived here from many planets, many galaxies and many solar systems that are so far unknown to Earth scientists. Although some of you journeyed here **seemingly** as sole individuals in quest of immortality that can only be achieved through the process of growth, you did in fact arrive not only accompanied by a specific number of Spirit Guides, but also by those Star Keepers from your home Universe.

Too much time and energy is wasted by people here particularly those who study the planetary systems "searching for intelligent life outside of this planet," and not enough time is spent, if any at all, regarding the study and acceptance of the fact that part of the intergalactic relationship with Earth is happening all the time through the interaction of the human race and Earth. Each world that exists within each Universe can be seen but erroneously identified as a "star." In truth however, if you were up close and personal with those seen as merely other stars, you would find worlds flourishing and evolving and many of them doing so at an astonishing pace. You see, one of the issues the Creator, the other Luminescents and I discussed **so long ago,** was what great benefit the soon-to-be manifested Earth Star planet would receive through a harmonious exchange of Souls from so many different galaxies. Although that was during the initial planning stages and still had to pass through the Creative processing state, Our agreement was unanimous. We believed those Souls could all work together to advance interstellar relationships while birthing new people here who would, could and should, have learned much from their elders. As a result the human races, <u>all of them,</u> would give unified births to ideas and ingenious realities that would advance all civilizations on all worlds equably and exponentially. I have tried so earnestly to carefully explain to all of you in previous messages that there is so much more to living life here on the planet than any of you realize. *The more you thought you knew, the less you actually did know.* I have further tried to explain that the more easily you each arrived at the realization that your very <u>differences</u> in beliefs and your vast misunderstanding about true reality are but products of your conditioning here and your misguided manner of believing in manmade reality figments and unilluminated illusions. Tell Me Children, can I possibly be any more clear about this?

While you are digesting those words, let Me ask you a question. Does anyone ever wonder about outer-galactic relationships and their effect on anything? They do exist you know. Or perhaps you do not know. My human Children only seem to want to discuss or even think about the facts purportedly stated as truth by scientists and professors and astronomers. Outer-galactic relationships stem from the great necessity of being able to always Create new and better worlds. These are the worlds that *coexist* in a beautiful balance of accrued knowledge, wisdom and the Soul desire of each life form to advance in a steady progression, in order to achieve a *final* return to Source. When a Soul arrives at that point it is then that the Soul can begin to live as a true INTEGRATED aspect of a Luminescent. It does not really matter if the Luminescent is MySelf or a God or Goddess from another galaxy, another faraway world. *What matters is that it must happen. Eventually.*

Meanwhile, back to the Earth Star planet; because there were many Souls who had not earned a respite from having lifetimes here, they were of course sent here again, or at times some Souls requested a return here as a means for self-atonement prescribed by the individual Soul itself. The expiation I am speaking of is not at all like what you may have once believed. It is a petition signed by a Soul and sent to High Council. It contains the Soul's desire to return to this planet as a means of possibly clearing up perhaps a karmic situation, or expunging old wrongdoings.

Our desires were that the ones who had need to be here...repeatedly if necessary...would be able to alter their previous life circumstances and gather together with goodhearted people of all races and thus overcome their previous Spiritual handicaps. Obviously, that did not then and still has not now worked out the way We desired. *"We"* in this sense, are the united whole of all who are the

Luminescents, the Creator and the Creation Processing. Unfortunately unlighted and belligerent people whose Soul Voices had faded from their memories began the purulent process of teaching untrue hypotheses based upon THEIR OWN realities and effectively "feeding through encouragement" weaker minded individuals to do the same. These main perpetrators lived vicarious lives of self aggregation. They could not and would not consider service to others as a lifestyle. So, on the one hand you had the unilluminated SOURCES and their LEGION painstakingly stalking the Souls who they perceived could easily be coerced into stumbling and falling. And on the other hand you had the people themselves whose very wills to succeed despite all odds, who were the ones that were simply giving up and giving in.

I have told you all many, many, times that each world reverberates with the thoughts, actions and non-actions of its inhabitants. So it can not be any wonder to you why the Earth has rebelled and now longs for **and shall receive her place in the Sun.** I have discussed previously with you the deleterious effects all races here have had on the Earth. What so many of you still fail to realize YET, is that so many of those I term, *the Watchers,* are here among you whether you are consciously aware of them or not. Where do they come from, some of you wonder. I can tell you that they each come from <u>your own home planets.</u> Just as their name implies, they watch and record. They then continuously transmit all the data they receive back to their own home planets. It is in this manner that others may learn or relearn if necessary, how a simple act of intentional unkindness, abuse and even thoughtlessness itself, can and does impact upon all life forms here and of course on Terra herself.

What was so long ago planned to be a grand joint venture and reunification process here on Earth, had well before the middle ages even began here, deteriorated into such a state of disease and dismay that Our plans for what We had once thought to be the perfect Earth have now been changed. It shall still take place, but in a non-linear epoch, after My NESARA Child completes her task here. I will be speaking of the unity and complete cooperation between My Star Keeper Children on other worlds and their own intergalactic relationships and their combined effect on and for Earth in a later chapter.

Celest... Well God, I can not begin to think of what questions to ask here. You managed to say a lot in a little bit of time. You stated that even the unilluminated Children wonder briefly about where they came from. Could you expand on this more please? Also, I believe readers would benefit more from "the process of growth" you mentioned, if you explained it more fully. You also said, "there is so much more to living life here than you know," or words to that effect, more explanation please. And lastly, how much if at all, have your own desires for the future of the evolvement of the human race changed?

God... And you said that **I** managed to say a lot in a little bit of time, *so have you Celest!* Ok, there are times that yes, the unilluminated Children do wonder where they came from; I sometimes see quick glimpses in their minds as a touch of curiosity overcomes their conditioned learning of *never to question,* for that is forbidden by those who hold these peoples' minds in captivity. Still, as long as they are walking in human form, they do sometimes become avidly inquisitive. This passes quickly however. They have for the most part been told they are part of an invincible army, a force of ONE. Furthermore, that they come from a planet that is inhabited only by all others who are like them. They have at times been convinced that the god they speak with is the only real god and that all other entities are its enemies. In time, if they live long enough here, nothing can convince them otherwise. So they engage in rapture-like binges; absolutely sure that they must follow their instructions or face a devastating and painful loss of life. These people have become legends in their own minds. So it is that the people who do not or can not survive are the casualties of their own disbeliefs. No, they do not see themselves as Souls anymore. To do so would give credence to the fact that *I exist.*

Celest, as you yourself know, the process of growth is of extreme importance. It is but <u>one</u> reason why you are who you are and WHY you are here. When I speak of this type of growth, what I am describing is a type of a usually slow maturation process that is a combination of ancient knowledge, innate wisdom and countless life experiences that eventually culminate into a Soul in <u>full bloom.</u> No, this process can not be hurried; it must achieve a state of fruition predicated upon ability, Spiritual agility and the sole desire for the Soul to be all that it can be **without limit.** As this process accelerates however, then the Soul must assure the personality that the individual must learn patience with events that must take place. You see, it is not enough to KNOW what must or will take place, the necessity here is KNOWING when to step back and allow things to happen without anyone's interference, regardless of how good their intentions may be. Yes, Celest, I do realize and completely understand why it is so difficult for Souls such as yourself and David to wait out long periods of linear machinations while knowing full well all situations that must be addressed and feeling restless and anxious waiting for the events to take place that **you know** will. I also empathize with you both and others who are like you, for the long and harsh periods of "doing without" that you experience. Yet, I do know that you both see how all those responsibilities and experiences ultimately favor your missions in the long run.

No, I do not fully expect all other Children to understand what I am saying about "the process of growth." But I do expect them all to respect the fact that *I* value its importance and that *I* know many things about this matter that they do not. "Maturity" exists on many levels. However, young Souls are not known to readily adapt to the patience process. It is NOT because of their stage of evolution, it is because they usually lack the prior experiences that function as great teachers.

Ok now, yes, I intentionally made the statement "**there is so much more to living life here than you know,**" I decided to dangle a carrot in front of everyone's eyes in an attempt to see how many readers would immediately seize upon that statement and question themselves about it. I am happy to say, *it worked.* You who are the Earthbound Children have such wonderfully fertile minds; now if I can only get you all to use that fertility rather than have that energetic mass deteriorate and become barren! Although I will speak in depth about this in a future book, I will touch upon it for now in order to give you something to think about. In one sense this world was a great experiment on Our parts. We provided the ways and means for a succession of "ages" to take place here that were intended to give you each better lives with more advanced technology. More for you **to grow** with. You were intended to alter past karmic situations by how you lived in the present and to rectify old animosities that you had with others from other civilizations and other past life experiences. Instead of this happening, those Children who were the stronger because of their acts of ruthlessness, depraved indifference for Spiritual matters and their continuous onslaughts of violence against the "weaker" but more Spiritual people, cast a penumbra over most minds and hearts that has lasted for many a lifetime. The Children who once knew about *life after life,* and *death through dishonor,* entered into a state of unawareness. Even though they did know AT ONE TIME, all that life truly incorporates, they left this knowledge in the dark recesses of their minds. As I stated earlier, I will speak on this matter more fully at a different time in a different book.

Well Celest, your last question is a bit of a mixture of possibilities and probabilities regarding the future existence of the human race. Because of the unique situation each of Us who are the Luminescents find ourselves in, it would be virtually impossible for any of Us to even consider the possibility of eliminating any life forms in any worlds, for any reason at all. So, because the human races have been devolving at an alarming pace for the last several centuries, I decided to simply allow them the dignity of falling and failing as much as they chose to, **until** the advent of NESARA and the Golden NOW. I decided that if the Children wanted to learn from painful experiences, then who was I to interfere? Devolvement is an interesting experience of and in itself. It always seems to be that only when a vessel has completely emptied can it then be purified and filled anew. I am in complete realization of the fact that My desires for the human race to advance and use their former worn-out life foundations as a vague memory to remind them of what not to do in the future, can be the new stepping stone to their new future life here. I also know that the new races of people here will spring forth bathed in LIGHT and living loving and productive lives. Of course this shall not happen overnight. Celest, why don't you wait for **100 years** and then ask Me if I am pleased with their individual and collective progress. Many iconoclastic people are already beginning their slow but steady emergence here. This pleases Me greatly. Their numbers will grow and develop a magnitude of *incandescent* power that will seem to be shocking to more timid minded people. This emergence that is slowly developing here will clearly be seen gathering people together of both sexes and from all cultures. No, these are not radical people in the sense of being violent. They are radical in the sense of insisting on and clamoring for, the advancement of themselves as true free human beings. They will attract more and more people for **the next 100 years.** Each person who feels the magnetic pull to join with these large groups will benefit greatly in strength of mind and staunchness of Spirit.

It gives Me the greatest pleasure and unlimited joy to share this news with each of you. So dear Celestial Blue Star, your own good works are also attracting these ones I speak of. You, and all the others like you, shall also reap the rewards that I once tried to give to the former generations. This is all I choose to say about this.

Celest... Thank you, God, for being YOU.

God (*received by David*) Today I want to discuss your relationships, not only the ones you have with one another, more importantly the relationships you each have with the galaxy you reside within. Each planet carries its own energy signature, its own personal vibration. Your astrologers' touch upon this briefly, but they do not have all the answers. The conjunctions, the alignments for example, of the planet most definitely impacts upon the Earth Star in many ways. The most important part of this for you right now, is how they interact with the energy fields surrounding this world. You see, there are a great many Earth changes ongoing at this time. These changes in many ways have never before been seen on this orb. As Terra continues to alter her realignment even more and to move her physical body into the higher frequencies, the planet herself will be affected by the magnetic pull from all the other stars and planets. Each of the other planets will continue to be affected as well, because of the monumental surge of energies. The shifts that you see in the Earth's crust are not on a collision course with Earth herself. As she continues to change her life situation, so will your moon do so and the others planets orbiting around the sun. You are seeing evidence of this in your media as they note the new discoveries and the shifting of the surface of these other planets. Now you will be feeling their impact upon Earth.

I want to caution you, none of what you have previously been taught applies any longer. This world is having a major transformation; one that has been eons in the making. Her landmasses will reformat as in times past; her bodies of water will shift. What you once *used* to consider being safe havens, isolated sections of the planet that had relatively moderate temperatures may no longer be so.

Other notable changes are the weather patterns. As NESARA continues her spiraling journey around and around this world, you will see great changes in not only the temperature, average rainfall and snow packs, you will be embracing winds that will seem to never cease. This is in great part due to the magnetic pull from the other celestial bodies. Other reasons for this are the extreme need to root out the remaining pockets of negativity which have held this planet in a form of Spiritual stasis and lackadaisical thoughts. This world has been in a holding pattern; awaiting the correct timeline when the mass consciousness would elevate to a level of the newly developed collective consciousness, that would allow some, not all, of Earth's inhabitants to flow along with her rather than away from her. The changes to your atmosphere are a much needed, natural cleansing of the elements which make up this world. Long have the resources of this world been defiled, however not nearly as much as they have over the last two centuries. The displacement of certain minerals and liquid materials from the crust of this world has contributed to a shift in her axis. No, there is nothing you can do to alter this; you can however help to minimize its effects. I want each of you to consider what it is you do every day, how you live your life and the sum total of whatever it is that defines your personal worlds. See where you can cut back on the consumption of resources; see where you can become more self-sufficient, without adding to the problem. There are natural ways of growing foodstuffs that work in harmony with soil, the air and the rest of the environment. Utilize the knowledge you have at your fingertips. Learn to be one with this world and she will respond in kind. She knows as We do that there are many parts of this planet that will not survive the coming changes. As the populations change, so will the landmasses in those areas, that is providing the changes BY the people are the positive ones. Understand now, if the people do not enact proper change, the landmasses will continue to be altered into new forms of themselves and AWAIT the generations of incoming Souls who are destined to be the new gardeners and protectors of this planet. Now, how does all this relate to your intergalactic relationships? Very simply stated, what you do to reinforce this world is your small, but extremely important part of your relationship with the Universe.

I know many of you are in awareness of all of which I speak, parts of these messages are intended to stimulate the minds and hearts of those who are not yet as awake as you are. These messages are to also remind you to consider how you can best be of service to this world and simultaneously be doing My work. That is why you are here, is it not? This world was never designated the playground for the lazy and aimless, it is not to be considered a place for Universal vacationers. Not yet anyway. In time it will be a place of respite for those who are in need of an infusion of Earth's loving touch while they are embracing her natural beauties and wonders. Let us move on shall we? Your desires for some form of *first contact* have brought many of My Star Keeper Children here at your own request. They are not here to pamper you, entertain you or to ultimately undo the damages you have done. That is your job. Their relationship with you is one of personal desire to assist their Earth cousins in finally lifting the veils that have shrouded your minds and hearts. Their desires stem from the bond of love that exists between family members, and you ALL are their relations. You might as well come into acceptance of that fact if you still believe that your race was completely Created as a singularity. Yes, the human race is unique, it was designed in many ways be one of the next steps in evolution. Your races were intended to co-join with everyone from every other benevolent world so they could come and join in. We did not break the mold after We made you, We would never destroy something that has been perfected. So, what can you do to help your fellow man through this apparently eerie transition? Most certainly do not hold their hand.

They have had as much time as any of you to decide for themselves what is right and true. The decisions must be up to the individual whether to continue riding the gravy train of Earth's past, or jump on the Golden Now express.

Ok, now, let Me briefly touch upon the relationships with the microcosmic as well as the macrocosmic. Each microbe that is brought to another world, each one that is unintentionally introduced into a controlled environment, has made changes far below a cellular level. The impact upon the people or environment can be seldom positive. I do not believe in good and bad, there is however the good and the not so good. Take for example the meteorites which have found their way to this planet. Some carried with them properties that were to be a benefit if used properly, for this world's inhabitants. Others carry certain microbes that are foreign to the human body's systems and thus would induce a state of bodily unrest, generally considered by each of you as disease. This relationship can alter the course of an evolutionary path. To make this clearer, I ask that you compare it to the dead zones within your oceans and waterways. What was once a naturally clean and perfectly designed entity has now been contaminated by outside influences. Although you see this in your water, you most certainly read about the pollutants which have contaminated the soil in many areas, and of course there is the ill-conceived nuclear waste byproducts which are contaminating the air, water and soil and all human life.

To bring this into a larger picture, envision what we have just discussed and put it into a Universal scale. Let us talk about your relationships with other worlds, many of which you have yet to physically come into contact with. What happens on the Earth Star planet impacts on all the other worlds, all the stars, in fact it affects all the other Universes. This is but one reason why the Gods and Goddesses of the other Universes are keeping a keen eye on the progress being made on this world. One dramatic shift in consciousness can alter the orbit of the spheres in the same galaxy. This in turn affects the natural rotations of all the corresponding galaxies and Universes. Many of you think that just because you have a thought, that it is yours and yours alone. This simply is not true. What comes around goes around. What comes into your minds goes out and around and around connecting with all similar thought patterns. This gives a seeming innocent thought power and momentum. Of course all of this is dependent upon how much *like attract like* energies of the same pattern, are out there for the thought to join with. So you see, while My Children from other worlds are impacting upon your world, in ways that are commonly misunderstood by you, you are affecting their worlds as well. What you do or think, how you relate to any circumstance or occurrence, is being cataloged and referenced and shared with those who study the information collected by those We term "the watchers." The watchers are the ones who monitor everything that occurs on a specific world, as well as everything that impacts upon **this** world originating from outside sources.

Now before I take My leave of this godumentary I wish to touch upon the influence certain other races of beings have had on this world, both negative and positive. As many of you know by now, your governments have been working in collusion with several other races of beings in hopes of gaining new technologies. I do not feel a need to remind you of their origins as this information is well documented all over your internet services. Since this nefarious relationship began your world has altered technologically and in many ways has lowered the consciousness of many of the people in this world. They no longer have to think for themselves. Technologies have enhanced your world, unfortunately many have been misused. Now instead of fighting amongst each other with bows and arrows, swords and spears, you now have laser weapons, remote controlled drone planes and machines that can turn the weather into a weapon to use against each other. These technologies were always available for you to use, they were never intended to be used against each other. If you could only remember your times on Atlantis and Mu, as well as the many other previous advanced human civilizations here on this world, then you would remember how the inappropriate use of such technologies led to the end of those civilizations... worldwide.

You may be living more comfortably now, you no longer have to use a chamber pot during the night, now that you have running water and indoor plumbing. In many ways even the poorest amongst you are living better now than the kings and queens of merely 100 years ago. The beings that traded the technologies for some of your greatest inventions such as the microwave, the computer chip and propulsion systems, did not do so because they had your best interests at heart. They did so because they knew that once you had a taste of what they could offer, you would only want more and more. They deceived you and they are still using you to get what they want. They do not care about you; you are a means to an end. They need you to survive; they need your planet's resources to satisfy their needs. Where this relationship will ultimately go is up to each of you. It can carry on for another fifty or one hundred years or you can use your collective voices to change the course of history here in the present. Your infrastructures are very fragile as they currently are and will not last much longer. Much of what is currently taken for granted will soon no longer be. You, as a collective, need to decide NOW where it is you will go from here. Your *possible* versus *probable* relationships with civilizations from other worlds are dependent upon this.

And I bet you thought I was going to use this chapter of "God Talk" to speak about Celest and David's intergalactic relationship and how it is impacting upon planet Earth. That should all be readily apparent to all of you by now. Good day.

David... Well God, as you know I always receive my message from you and then I go back and read what you had to say to Celest for her part. I wonder how many people are going to have a hard time believing that first of all, Souls from everywhere venture here to Earth for a life experience and secondly, how many other people will there be who are going to have a hard time understanding how it is that so many of their Guides and those from their home worlds journey here with them. And that they all are here for the duration of an incarnation. It would seem like a long time and a serious commitment on the *others* parts, especially when you take into consideration how most Earthizens relate to space travel and the amount of time it takes to get from say, here to the moon. Any comments?

God... First of all, the kinship that exists between those that consider themselves to be "family" knows no bounds. There is no separation about their relationships in their minds, not even through time or matter. When a commitment is made it is of no inconvenience to *be there* for another, you yourself have done this many lifetimes over. Many of those who have been with you before, are here yet once again. Space travel is not completely understood here on the Earth, not yet anyway. What may take you months of travel time to accomplish can be done by most civilizations almost instantaneously. As far as the amount of time a guardian requires, this is of no consequence when you consider the limitations surrounding a linear experience. As you well know, the Earth is the only place where it was deemed necessary to instigate a measure of linear time. The more anyone begins to first understand and then exist within the limitlessness non-time that is part of living in the NOW, then they will realize that it is no burden at all. Each of these Souls that journeyed with their charges can go back home any time they want for a little respite and be back before the charge awakens from their *downtime*. I have already addressed the matter defining why so many Souls from other galaxies and solar systems venture here, so I will not repeat MySelf except to say, the Earth Star Walk is considered to be a major challenge for many. As such it entices them and it beckons to them on a level that can only be felt, not shared. How's that?

David... Works for me. I have the advantage of *knowing* most of what you just explained and I do understand how easy it is to **go home** for a night to be with family. Thank you.

God Talk 10

The Tomorrows beyond the Todays

God *(received by David)* This may well be the chapter that many of you will jump ahead to in this book to see what it is I have to say. I counted heads in the previous *"And Then God Said..."* book and there were so many of you that read the 2012 chapter before even bothering with the introduction, that I actually almost lost count. It happened again in *"Beyond the Veil ~ Epiphanies from God,"* when so many readers jumped ahead to the chapter, "New book of Revelations." What this tells Me, is that there are still too many of you who want to know what the end result will be before you have completely understood the sequence of events that must precede the final event. Far too many of you still believe that you alone cannot influence coming events. This is sad, you have the **Power of Creation** within you and you are reluctant to utilize this Divine gift to its fullest potential. It is time for you to reprogram that aspect of your mind, for *if* you are to succeed in this lifetime, you must be willing to go through the repetitive, sometimes tedious process of personal and planetary ascension, one step at a time. If not you may stumble and fall, I would certainly not like to see that happen to you *especially* when you are so close to crossing the finish line. Some of you can take quantum leaps, this is true. Here is an analogy for you: even those few who are capable of this feat still must be able to understand that it is the consistency of the dough that determines the quality of the donut. If it is too thick it will become lumpy and not taste right. If it is too thin it will not have the stability needed to maintain itself and it may break or fall apart leaving an inferior final product. Now that We have the baking lesson out of the way, let Us proceed on to the heart of this chapter. By the way, the composition of the dough (which are experiences had and lessons learned **and understood**) constitutes the makeup of the donut, (the completed you.)

I am in awareness of the fact that many of you are putting forth so much effort to disguise the fact that you are trying to slide under My radar. Do you really believe that I would not notice that some of you are doing *just enough* to keep your foot in the door? And that you are doing so *just in case* everything I have told you about personal and planetary destinies aligning with this planet's decision to evolve **with or without you,** does somehow end up being the truth? Do not for a moment think that I will let any of you complete this lifetime without giving it your all, especially when it comes to finishing your missions here. Evolution is a steady stream of progressive movements. The timeline you are now in is infinitely too important to begin grading any of you on a sliding scale. Either you have what it takes and have learned your lessons well and <u>applied</u> what you have learned, to the best of your abilities, or you will not ride with Terra upon the wings of My NESARA. There are no more free rides; there are still an amount of tickets available but each must be earned day in and day out. Now before you start doubting yourself I ask that you ask yourself one simple question, <u>are you doing your best</u>? How you answer this question will either reassure you that you have earned the right to call yourself a true human being in activated God I AM form, or you haven't. Simply stating you are a Light Worker and then going about your life without having anything of substance to back it up will no longer do, in fact it never did. The only one you are fooling is yourself. If I have offended any of you perhaps you should ask yourself why? If you think I am being too harsh please tell Me now. It will not change My stance but it will show Me that you have taken a STAND. I admire that. I do not expect all of you to believe everything I say, I DO expect those of you who don't to tell Me why.

As we come closer to the conclusion of this book I would like to sum up for you some of the information which I deem to be of importance to all of you who are looking to the future with great anticipation. I caution you, it will not be all sunshine and roses, nor will it be all doom and gloom. In the next few decades you will be bearing witness firsthand to some of humanity's cruelest moments, as their needs are no longer met. Their animosity towards one another will increase its feverish tempo as the layers of illusions, their security blankets, are stripped away leaving them only their primal instincts to satisfy their desires. The immature, emotionally unbalanced, Spiritually devoid "have-nots" will want more, and they will take it if they can. The so-called "haves" will be astonished to find out that what they once deemed to be of importance to them, will no longer sooth the hunger pains and shelter them from the coming storm. Some will choose to give up, throwing their hands up in the air in utter despair. Others will attempt to hold onto their status in society not knowing that these positions no longer exist. I urge you all to try to remain calm; keeping your wits about you, may well be your saving grace.

In the days ahead many of you will be privileged to witness firsthand the fruits of your labors as they come into partial if not full manifestation. I know that many of you are reaching the end of your current life cycles, and that is ok. Thanks to you the ball is now rolling in the right direction. None of you who are adults now will be alive to see all the changes take place. Many of you have done what you agreed to, for the most part, and assisted this world out of the darkness her physical body had descended into. I thank you for that. It could have been done without you; however it has always been much easier to accomplish something of this magnitude by working together. The people of this world will never know, at least not in this lifetime, just how close the human race came to extinction. If I were able to reach out to all the people directly and tell them the truth I still do not believe that many of them would change their ways. Sadly, it is not in their nature to do so without great resistance. You yourself have had to learn, however painfully it may have been at first that you cannot save another from their own fate. You did learn that it was not your place to do so. You also learned how difficult a simple little thing like remaining passionately detached can be. No, it is not easy to see so many bad things happening all around you and knowing that it is not your place to deprive another person of an experience.

Together you and I will walk hand in hand into the future, embracing all that the Golden Now has in store for us. I said Now, not "age." The NOW is forever. I do not know exactly how <u>everything</u> is going to play out in the days ahead. I do know that everything will change for the better, that has been foreseen by Us long ago. The people of this world are now being forced to confront themselves and few are really ready to accept that responsibility. This is why so many of Earth's citizens will be leaving this world in search of other opportunities for them to, no pun intended, see the light. The blame game for this world's unnatural behavior will continue until it has run its due course. Eventually, those who are still left Standing will have to join together and rebuild this world and learn from the experiences of the many dynasties about what went wrong. What could have been and should have been different will then be understood. Then We will get together and begin rebuilding this world as a new world, beginning at the ground floor. I hope you will all join Me here, in one form or another.

This world is rapidly becoming ripe in ways you do not yet understand and ready to start bearing fruit. She only needs a little more from you; she needs you to continue sprinkling your Spiritual waters upon her body. You all know how to do this. Spiritual water in this sense is the inner essence, the Light that you emit from within. When focused with only the best of intent, it **will** begin the germination of the seeds you have all planted along the way. I would imagine that most of you never considered yourselves to be farmers. Well, I am asking you to become what you are, the *patient* gardeners, the attentive caretakers of this world and please, this time around do so with purpose. In other words, let there be no more hurried slapdash decisions. I am trying to encourage you to examine **each** decision you make and treat it as if it were the most important one of your life. What you do from this point on, how you devote yourself to your *chores*, will shape all of your tomorrows to come. Do not take this lightly, for I am gifting you with *a pearl of wisdom* that has long been in the making.

After today and consequently every day which is to follow, I will be asking more of you than you ever imagined you had in yourselves to give. We will be working countless numbers of long days and often throughout the night comparing notes, planning, orchestrating and implementing the changes WE, you and I, deem to be of great importance. First and foremost will be the comforting and rehabilitating of the tired and weary who are still left standing. In order for this to work everyone must be involved. In our late night deliberations We will be examining everything that went wrong before, so that We as a collective, do not make the same mistakes again. When We are finally finished We will all gaze fondly upon this... OUR HOME....with parental pride!

I realize that the title of this chapter can be a tad bit misleading *for as We all know*, tomorrow never really comes, for it is always today. This is what living in the Now is all about. What you do today opens the door to your next today. So one might say and with great truth I might add, that right here, right now IS the most important moment of your lives. And when you are done with this one, then the next one will present itself. It is hard to impress upon you the immense importance your decisions in the present are to you, they can make all the difference in shaping our tomorrows. You do not have the benefit of being able to completely step outside of yourself and see how every sequential scene plays out, one right after another after another. If you were able to then you would see how all the pieces of your life fit neatly together.

Each Soul who is blessed enough to be here now has the unique opportunity to not only be of service to his or her fellow humans, they have the absolute responsibility to use the gifts they possess to help rectify the wrongs and injustices done *in the name of progress* to all aspects of this world. There are millions upon millions of life forms that desperately **need** your undivided attention now if they are to survive. Do not engage in favoritism of one over another, each are equally important. You see, it is not just the planet and the human race We are trying to save here, it is also *every*thing else. Over planting of forests is causing as much damage to the environment as is deforestation. The

Earth knows when the natural order in an area needs to be maintained. Fire is a great cleanser in this regards. There must always be a balance maintained in each part of an eco system. There are many areas of this world where the human element has infringed upon nature's natural selection process. Maintaining a balance in the food chain is critical to sustaining and maintaining equilibrium among the species. There are parts of this world that are in the process of undergoing major changes, much of this will be accomplished through an accelerated, unbiased purification program. This process will not be limited to fires, floods, tornadoes, hurricanes and the like. You are about to observe planetary events occur that your best fiction writers have not even dreamt of yet. These *shifts* will be orchestrated by the planet herself. She knows better than any of you which parts of her have been overstressed by the human hand of greed and insecurity.

Terra will do what is necessary to bring completion to the ever repetitive cycle you had her captured in. You as a collective can alleviate much of this cycle by altering your perspectives about how you rate/value the importance of each aspect of this world. I cannot tell you which areas will be hardest hit, for that is up to each of you to decide through your actions and underlying motives. I can tell you that a vast number of My Star Keeper Children are <u>at this</u>

very moment evaluating every square inch of this world, not just the planet's most distressed areas. During the evaluation process they are taking everything into consideration when determining whether certain areas can still be preserved/saved. Nothing pertaining to these evaluations is written in stone, but as My good friend Blue Star the Pleiadian recently said, "I would start praying for those areas that you feel strongly about, while you still can, Africa being one." If you do not take this on yourself to do this, these areas may be lost forever. Continental shifts have happened in the past and there is no reason for you to believe they will not happen again. There is so much unnecessary pain and suffering going on everywhere. Do what you can to alleviate it, each tiny act of kindness will magnify itself more than you realize. Stop turning a blind eye to those around you. There are no longer enough food stuffs in today's turbulent climate to feed the ever-changing populations of this world. You must *never* choose one race or culture of people over another; you *must* choose to treat each equally, without bias or discrimination. Most of you have not done this *as a collective,* for as long as the Earth Star has graciously hosted you. Now it is time for you to turn over a new leaf, to open a new chapter in your humanitarian pursuits. Children of this world, both young and old, I encourage you to embrace being young at heart, see each other as I do, as the Gods and Goddesses you all are. Rise above your petty differences and work together for the common good, while there is still time to do so. If you do, the tomorrows which lie beyond the todays, will be brighter and you will naturally become more optimistic about the future. Also, <u>the pantries of your Soul will be filled with abundance</u>. Do you not believe this is so?

To those who are working on the premise that there are fewer tomorrows left before you than those that lie behind you. let Me remind you that you DO have *This Day* to choose to make a positive difference in your life and the lives of others. Start with something small, think kindly of yourself, speak to your plants or just simply help someone with their groceries. Each of these are Light filled pursuits. When you harvest the fruits from your trees and bushes, leave some for your four legged friends and those who flutter from above. Speak with the soil beneath your feet, wiggle your toes in it and then ask Terra what you can do to make it fertile and lush once more. See, know, understand, and learn to read the signs. You can no longer afford to abuse the soil by over farming. The dustbowl days during the great depression are knocking upon your doors once again. If you do not wish a repeat of those hardship days long gone by, then I suggest you take preemptive measures RIGHT NOW, for it is almost too late to stave this one off. If this is allowed to transpire because you individually and as a race did nothing to stop it, then you have no one to blame for the hardships which are to follow. Clean usable water is another great concern. Your irrational abuse of this precious natural resource can no longer be tolerated. It is up to you to stand up for IT's rights while you still can. Water cannot defend itself from the abusive practices you as a race have generated. It can and has shown you that it has no master. Left to its own devices it will take many a year for it to be able to run clear and free once again. Remember what you have seen, so that no one will ever have to revisit this era in human history again. I am being reminded by the Creator to mention to each of you that this world is your home, if you allow it to wither into decay then you may well be the instrument that orchestrates your own demise.

"Today IS the first day of the rest of your lives," you have heard this before so this is nothing new. What is new is that some of you are actually taking the time to consider what this truly means to you. Stop thinking about your mortality and get a life instead. You have died a physical death many times before and were reborn, there is no reason for you to believe that this time around will be any different. This pull, this inner feeling so many of you experience, is a sense of urgency being prompted by Soul in

order for you to rapidly pick up the pace about what it is you are here to accomplish. Time may feel as if it is accelerating and rightly so. You must utilize every waking moment to fulfilling your destinies, for before you know it *the opportunity* may well have passed you by. You do not want this and I most certainly do not want to see you waste a single favorable opportunity that is available for you to accomplish all that you can in this or any other lifetime. In the tomorrows beyond the todays, the world around you will appear to be in utter chaos and in truth it will be. The difference this time around, from **all** the previous times, is that this is ORGANIZED CHAOS. There is a difference. You can *and should* thank the Creator and the Creation for that one.

David... I am curious if to hear from You if approximately two-thirds of Earth's current human population will be transitioning off this planet, then what will become of all the homes, businesses, cars etc.? Certainly not everyone is going to be needing three homes and five cars.

God... Good question David, one that I know you already have the answer for. Most will be reabsorbed, recycled, or simply cease to be. This world, despite what most may believe, takes the refuge from your waste sites and reprocesses it. So you see, other than your toxic waste, everything is capable of being reused in one form or another. I have told you previously that nothing is ever lost or discarded, everything is energy, vibrating at one frequency or another. It is a simple matter, although many among you may relate to it as *a sleight of hand movement,* although there are no parlor tricks here, to alter the vibration of a substance and then transform it into something that is of use. Certainly there must be some of you who still remember the old stories of *turning water into wine* or *lead into gold,* that have been passed down from generation to generation.

Thankfully the time of needing five bedroom homes, six car garages and 1.2 children are at an end. Keep this in mind as you are rebuilding this world, keeping things simple and lightening your loads will free your minds and hearts and allow you the freedom to find personal satisfaction in areas you never before thought possible. The only limitation is your imagination, use it well.

David... Obviously one of the questions on many people's minds is what is going to happen with the currencies of the world. Any comments?

God... My question for them is, *do you believe there is still a need for them*? David, you know as well as I do that the value of anything is only what you individually place upon it. Soon there will no longer be anyone with a need or desire to control/manipulate commerce, everything will transform and start to favor a new mechanism which <u>you the people,</u> will put into place to accommodate everyone's needs. For the time being, during the hopefully brief transitional stages, knowing how and what to barter with will be your greatest ally. Keep this in mind as you are rebuilding this world. There is nothing you need to bring from the old world into the new one, if it was not Created within a Light filled heart. Leave the past behind, consider this a SECOND CHANCE to get things right.

David... How long will it take for the oceans to become vibrant once again?

God... As long as it takes for the people of this world to swallow their pride and **ask** for help. Pride can either be an asset or a liability, the choice is yours. There is no shame in admitting you need help now and then, only a fool would believe they could do it all by themselves. The technology exists to repair the damage that has been done to this planet; I will speak more on this in a later book.

David... Thank you God. If anyone has any other questions, I believe they should just ask you directly.

God... Right you are David.

God *(received by Celest)* Everyone asks Me about "tomorrow." The Children want to know what to expect, when to expect whatever it is and how they will and IF they will benefit. Also, most people rather timidly ask Me if they will survive to experience "tomorrow." Although I choose to phrase My answers to each Soul differently, depending on how mature they are and how much truth they can handle, ultimately My answers are the same. The first thing I tell them is, *"if you want to see tomorrow, first you must get through today."* That never goes over very well with them! I don't know why....well, yes I do, but at times their desires for truth are rather muddled, to say the least. OK, at the risk of sounding repetitious, I will once again tell you that each of your today moments is but a mirror reflection of your tomorrows. NO, that does not mean that if you are having a day of low energy and anxiety attacks that it will simply resurface again tomorrow. Unless you want it to of course; also it MAY happen if you have not altered your current "conditions." It means that if you are one of the millions and millions of people here who are living lives that border on unhappiness or discontent with your life choices, then you must first *"clean up your act,"* before you receive a new mirror. You did not know that you each receive a **new** mirror each day that you change something important in your lives, now did you? Of course there are those people who for many reasons do not like to look into any mirror. Granted, mirrors are actually distortions of an image, any image. However, their true use is of far greater import than you once realized.

None of you Children have the capability of seeing yourselves as you truly are. So how in this world can you possibly expect to see the tomorrow, if you can not see the today? This not a rhetorical question, I assure you. As the constellations of yourselves, you have the gift of altering everything in your personal world by first deciding what is and what is not in your own best interest. You do not have to be My Nostradamus Child reincarnated and performing the ancient art of scrying to see what is the best reality for you and what is not. Look back over your lives please, if it is not too painful for you and see how you could have used your free expression to change circumstances that would have had a **good and healthy** domino effect on your previous tomorrows. Again and again and again, I and many of My finest teachers here, have warned all people not to allow certain experiences to outlive their usefulness. When their usefulness has been outlived, to dawdle further with them can only cause you great consternation and more confusion about why you had them in the first place. Think of each unhealthy and unrealistic experience you have had in your previous todays. All overactive involvements and overexposures to unhealthy or abusive events and people are not productive, to say the least. It is the sum total of those events that I ask you to consider. It is only through the consideration of those times that you can make an informed decision based upon prior knowledge that you DID once have, but did NOT use. Those "informed decisions" will be the ones for you to use without over-rationalization, in order for you to NOT repeat those previously ill-chosen experiences and events. You see Children; I gave all of you knowledge that you could easily re-acquire and re-acquaint yourselves with through your own sentience, rather than from any well-intentioned abstract reasoning. So why continue to subject your conscious self with the, *"I didn't know any better,"* train of thought? I believe the appropriate slang term here is..."*it's a cop-out.*"

A mirror, at least the ones I am telling you about that you each Create everyday, can be considered to be a byproduct of a consciousness that you are living <u>at that moment,</u> that is a type of a compilation of a present emotional and Spiritual state of being. As such it simply radiates outwardly what is going on with you inwardly. If you look in a mirror and all you can see are fine lines and tiny wrinkles then you are only seeing a distorted view of an outward reflection. This is one reason why so many people have a difficult time looking into a mirror. It is also why the mirror is holding the imprint that you have unconsciously set on it and MAY carry that over into future mirrors. That is sad indeed! I want to be very clear about this; time is required to set a new mirror into motion on a daily basis. So it is that much of what you think about during any given day or night is the catalyst for what you will see the next day. However, because so many people here have always been more worried about their **outer** appearance and constantly compare their own countenance to other people's looks, they miss the whole point of what the mirror really is symbolic of. I would very much like to see that change, you know. By the way, the symbolism I speak of is in actuality much more than merely emblematic. It is IN FACT an accurate representation of all aspects of an individual.

A mirror will change and upgrade itself as you yourselves upgrade your minds and Spirits. Obviously, I do not want to see any of you running around and singing **"Kumbayah,"** or acting more than a bit daffy as a means to alter your own conscious state. That would not be a good thing! Each of you who are now active participants in the collective consciousness will find, that is if you care to take the trouble to do so, that standing in front of a mirror and thinking about the good things that will happen in this world, will bring a shine and glow to your eyes and face as those thought-forms co-join with who it is that you are rapidly becoming. I use the term "rapidly" in a loose manner. To Me, yes, it is rapid; but of course to you it may seem to take "forever." All the many tomorrows that so many of you will have are of course an **integration,** it is a union of who you are, what you know and most importantly, *what you will do from this point on.* Although I do understand the vanity issue here, people on this planet simply do not want to age. However, if you do not grow old, then how can you become young again? Because there are now so many people who are changing all that they are able to in their today lives, these are the people who will find that although they will grow old, they will regenerate and continuously upgrade themselves in an unconscious manner. In other words, their Soul Selves will shine through in a more expansive and better way.

Ok, when I first began writing this particular chapter I saw Celest scratching her head and wondering where in the world I was going with this. In but a few minutes however I heard her silent "aha," and knew she understood why this had to be written. Oh MY dear wonderful Souls, it is time for you all to have a better understanding of this matter. If, just **if**, I am able to reach even 1% of you who are reading this chapter and see that My message here is either being understood or will soon be, then at the very least I will know that the ones who have the understanding can teach it to others and so on and so on. We, all of Divinity, see you each as you truly are sans makeup, Botox, or expensive clothes. We look for and find the real you; the matrix of **you** that so many of you Children have done your best to hide from. Unfortunately too many have succeeded. In order to sip from the elixir of life you must first be lead to this miraculous substance. Then you choose to sip or not to sip. This is a matter for your own free expression. The fact that I do know what to expect of each of you, even given the probability odds about the ones here that will fail themselves, of course makes it easy for Me to know how much your looking glass changes. *Looking glass* is definitely the better term. Think of the connotations to that, please.

I consider each of you who will now begin to use the looking glass in a productive fashion to be the true avant-garde Children who can and will see a better tomorrow and many tomorrows as well. Except for the fact that you each grade yourselves on how well you do with any venture, no one else will use a grading system as a means to define all your actions. Each of you who are intent on changing your lives will also find that a side of yourselves, the autonomous side, will begin to quicken in anticipation of every day beginning an entirely new chapter in your life. This will happen on both a conscious and SuperConscious level. *How long it will be for you to see the results?* As I said before, *it is entirely up to you.* No, Children, I am not saying that this all begins with the simple act of understanding and correctly using your mirrors. I **am** however saying that it is by the tried and true manner of learning about the truly important facts of life that you can then turn each new beginning, each new today, into an entire array of brilliant tomorrows. When you begin to truly live today, you will find that the Golden NOW will be ever-present to aid you. No one can simply go through life attempting to muster their strength and energies by living only in the everyday practical world. Those who do try to do this are very disappointed to find their todays to be EXACT replicas of all their previous todays and previous tomorrows. That is sad. *A mirror is a terrible thing to waste. Even worse, to lose.*

Celest... Now that we all know why you expressly stated that this is an important part of what people need to know and how the lack of understanding everyone has had about todays and tomorrows could easily impair their futures, would you please explain to everyone that the low energy days could be caused by outside influences too and how people should handle this while still maintaining their desire to use the mirrors?

God... Yes, I will do this Celest; let Me begin with the first part of your statement. Of course there are still outside influences running rampant here; although it is still not as overwhelming a horde as it was until only a few years ago. Parasites can not survive without hosts. This is elementary knowledge. Every entity, every species of life is intent on its own survival; therefore it is vitally important for them to feed off of whatever energy is available. Energy that My Children have can be very easily depleted from their consciousness without them having the knowledge that this is happening. When this occurs, yes, most definitely, it can easily result in both bouts of low energy for no "known" reason and unusual anxiety attacks. Also, the more empathic people on the planet far too easily tune into and pick up on other less balanced peoples' emotional distress and unhappiness.

The first way to deal with this situation is by first recognizing what it is. This falls under the *cause and effect* category. Once the determination has been made that whatever is happening is NOT something that you yourselves are doing wrong, then you can purge and sever that outside influence through the simply recognition factor. Do not FEED it or it will want to stay with you! I do want you all to understand that the more you immerse yourselves in the collective consciousness the more you will see miracles in action. The greater the incoming numbers of other people increases, I speak of those who will be anxious to join the collective, the more empathic this world shall become. Obviously as these numbers grow in sheer magnitude, the result will ultimately be that all those Children who are and those others who will be the survivors of disorganized chaos, and those who will readily adapt to organized chaos, will experience empathy as they never have before while they have been in mortality. No one shall lose their mirrors as long as they keep on trying to change what they can, especially in their own lives. The mirrors will not shatter just because you are having a low energy day, you know. What is of primary importance though is that you **each** not only recognize the truth that I am telling you about your mirrors, but that you should each also indulge in some *reflections* of how you can Create wonderful events in life and please, please, allow yourselves the privilege of understanding that with each newly Created event, something else equally wonderful is taking place. You see, as each Soul here refuses to be a participant with the harbingers of gloom and doom; as each Soul here adamantly chooses to believe that *they themselves as Soul can and will succeed,* yet another and another dark shadow will leave this planet. NO, not all of you may be aware of this part as it happens; however if you monitor yourselves you will find yourselves having more periods of "lightness and a sense of contentment." I am not saying those periods will last very long. **I am saying however,** that although they may be brief, they will consummate the union, the joining of you, yourself, as Soul walking in mortality, with the GREATER I AM.

The more often you experience those moments of joy, the more often they will return again and again, as the dark shadows walking in human form have no choice but to slacken their tenacious grip on humanity. Also, it is in this manner that your individual mirrors gather more strength and luminance. You see Children, the other part of this wondrous time is that as the collective consciousness grows stronger day by day as a result of the strengthening of your individual mirrors, in due time the collective will form a gigantic shield, a mirror composed of particles of each of your own mirrors and the Light that will emanate will be unstoppable. Do you see?

Celest... Thank you so much for your detailed explanation, God. One last question God; would please explain to everyone the full scope of "not seeing yourselves the way you truly are?"

God... Well, I don't know about giving everyone the full scope, there probably are not enough pages in this book. However, I will be detailed and try to say a great deal in a little bit of time. When I made that statement I was not referring to the Light you each bear. I was speaking on a practical world level. My human Children have a rather awkward tendency to compare themselves to others. Although they should be seeing themselves *in* others. All right, I will give a brief example of what I am referring to. If there are 100 people standing in a large room and all eyes are focused on just one individual, what do you think happens? All 100 people, yes including the person of interest, each formulate INDIVIDUAL assumptions of what that one person truly is like and how that person's physical appearance either jells or does not, with what each of the other people's ideas are of what it should be. The individual under the microscope even has their clothes analyzed; their hair style, the color of their hair and their facial features overall are scrupulously studied. These comparisons at times are merely random, yet at other times the "object" in question will be a well-known personality. Many people who indulge in this senseless exercise do so because of an ego based competitive streak they have. In this sense ego could be defined as either ego that is aggressive and unyielding, or one that is weak-minded and introverted. Children, it does not matter who you are; comparing yourselves to other people is a reckless and feckless abandonment of being sure, of being confident of your own independent life. Earthbound people are so reluctant to simply accept who they are, how they look, or feel, or think and thus do NOT apply value to their lives because they engage in this baneful attitude. These are inferior attitudes condoned by a life form species who were Created NOT to be inferior. Hmm, I am already hearing thoughts in many minds that are bordering on being appalled at the very idea that they are either comparing themselves to others, OR, *heaven forbid,* condoning that behavior. Well, I suppose I am not known as *the great illusion breaker* for nothing!

Yes, you all do this to some degree or another. If you feel that you must not give credence to this reality check I am giving you, then that of course is up to you. However, please bear in mind that I do **know** what you are thinking. As far as "condoning" this behavior is concerned; everyone who continues to "privately" grade themselves in this way, IS condoning this everyday occurrence. This is to a great extent why so many people must have the latest styles in clothes and accessories. On an unconscious level these people are trying to emulate someone else for fear of being ridiculed for just being themselves. I believe this sums it up for now.

Celest... Thank you, God.

God... Celest, I changed My mind. There is an issue I want to address here and now. I have spoken of the ability of the collective consciousness to erect a mirror that is a type of *shield*. I said that it is composed of particles of all of your own mirrors. I feel that if I do not explain one other part to this then I would not be giving you enough fact. The collective is a cosmic paradigm of various energies. It is for this reason that the importance of you each understanding not only the function of your own mirrors, but how they each relate to and with the collective is of such great consequence to your future and the future tomorrows as well. As the collective gathers more filaments of Light and more mirror particles from you each, it becomes a monolith, one that also functions as a catalyst for causing a disintegration of dark and unhealthy energy streamers. It is as this takes place that a barrage of Light MATTER infuses the collective from higher dimensions. That matter is a type of "blending agent." It has what I can only describe as an infinite web-like structure that works through the connectedness of the mirror fragments. In its own way it knits together more Light matter, and then fills any gaps or irregular pieces of mirror energies. It does so by formulating a pattern of Soul energies that contain the luminescence needed to ward off the dark ones. It is because of this endeavor that the dark is pushed further and further off planet. NO, this shield can not be destroyed; nor is it constricted. It is quite able to exist after the span of mortality of any human person has passed. This means that even when a person leaves their mortality and Soul adjourns to Nirvana, that precious bit of mirror bestowed upon the collective remains. The collective and the shield can not grow smaller; only larger. *That's it for now.*

Celest... Thank you God, I believe you were correct about needing to add the additional information.

God Talk 11

My Star Keeper Children

God*(received by Celest)* You should have all known that at one point or another in one of these books, I would choose to speak of My other wondrous Children who live on other planets, many in other Universes, who are ***Star Keepers***. This is the correct term for these Children. They are the Keepers of their Stars. Whatever star they live on is their planet. They are the guardians of these worlds they call "home." I, My Universe, the Creator and the Creation Processing, as well as all the other Luminescents from all other Universes, rely heavily on all the Star Keeper Children I am speaking of. Perhaps before I proceed further, this would be the proper place to speak of you who are the Earthbound Children, in relation to the Star Keeper races as a whole. I do believe I shall make this chapter longer than a few of My previous ones. Before the Earth Star planet was Created, those of you who were part of those former times and there are many of you here now who were, originated as Souls in other Universes as well as in My own. However, even though you may think of this planet Earth as aged she is in fact in her preteen stage, compared to other worlds that is. So it was and is that so many ancient civilizations in so many other Universes predate every civilization you know of here on this planet. Although I do have many, many, worlds within My own Universe, I am speaking mainly here of the others.

There have been ferocious wars fought on all worlds in all Universes as the goodhearted Souls who lived there engaged without choice, in battles against the "fallen ones." It was well-known that those fallen beings' main purpose in life was to capture and ultimately destroy all worlds that were not their own. On the other hand, the "Planetizens" who were the very core of their individual worlds, too had to begin in a Chrysalis state that initially began just as your own have. Each level arrived at in that earliest of development stages were precursors for the slow but steady evolution of all their own life forms. As each Soul entered a specific apex in their lives where they began to progress as a whole of ONE mind, One Spirit, the once slower pace began an enthusiastic march up the path, up the ladder of evolution. Because of those events, each time they reincarnated they were more apt to reestablish their Soul connection quickly. You see, I am not in any way saying they had it any easier than you have; however their free expression was fiercely bent on keeping their Soul status in forward growth movement while at the same time doing what they had to do to protect their home planets and all their lives. This is what I was referring to when I said,

"They engaged without choice in battles." They were all faced with life or death consequences if the unilluminated energies and their constant assaults on those worlds would have succeeded in their horrendous pursuits of planetary takeovers. It would not have stopped with just one planet; those hordes would have tried to consume every Universe.

These were also the entities who attempted to use deicide as a means of eliminating all Gods and Goddesses on all worlds. Obviously for reasons you should each understand, the deicidal plans had to be stopped before they could start. All good strategists are aware that in order to dominate and thus be in complete control of a populace, the main Care Takers or Overseers, must first be eliminated. None of Us ever underestimated those entities. We knew of their inherent ability to kill without reason and to viciously, **without conscience**, destroy worlds and capture Souls. I said, *without conscience,* because in truth they have none. So it came to pass that because all worlds begin in a more primitive state, much as your own did.....to some degree, each world developed a means of teaching all their people, especially young children about the dangers the incursive entities truly represented. Some planets did wage wars among themselves within their own worlds, until such time that they were **given** an unmistakable reality check by the prime Luminescent of their Universe.

That is when wars among themselves stopped and the Planetizens of those worlds began to understand the true nature of themselves. THAT too is a sign of Soul maturity.

Unlike the situations here on the Earth Star planet where young children are raised in illusionary concepts and then go on to become adults who steadfastly not only continually believed those broad abstract ideas, but also expanded upon them and taught others the same lies, other worlds learned early on to begin teaching the young as soon as possible This is how generation after generation of beings evolve in a finer, more natural way. No, I do not condone taking another's life; nor do any of the other Luminescents. We all do understand however that *to protect and serve* has more than one meaning. The saving grace for all Star Keeper races is their knowledge and understanding that although they will have to take another's life when absolutely necessary, the reincarnation process still is available for ALL those who fall. This way they can each know that someday, somewhere, those dark entities **may** choose to elevate themselves to a better station in their life through the utter dismissal of the desire to remain a part of a rapacious horde. It is further understood by the defending Star Keepers that it is NOT their responsibility to try to change an entity that has not yet shown any desire to change. Earthbound Children, if you had each had the opportunity during any of your previous life experiences on Terra to enter into a covenant of sorts, one that precluded the necessity of having to deal with such atrocious behavior by the lesser children, then YES, you would be living in a better time in the present time.

I am not saying that all the Star Keepers from other worlds and other dimensions did not have to deal with some "irrational" citizens living on their own worlds. That would be as truthful as the dastardly fable that many of you believe which is that *you are descendents of the apes.* Remember, all Souls first begin as Souls in training. THAT is a part of the true evolution of all life forms. Because of this "evolution factor," there have always been Souls who seek to remain at a lesser evolved state than do others. For those Souls on other worlds who choose this methodology as a means of experiencing only so much, many go on and work with others who have chosen the same station in their Soul lives. As Souls arrive at a critical timeline when they have need to go to other planets in order to learn more and possibly teach others as well, if they are not strong-willed enough, the possibility always exists that they could indeed become tainted by others who did not have the arriving Souls best interests at heart.

You see, as part of the Creation Processing event, there were worlds Created that were originally intended to house less evolved Souls. However as spatial understanding decreased among those particular Souls, they became more and more loath to participate as genderless Souls involved in the pursuit of evolution. In what would seem to you to be in no time at all, these Souls became intrigued by dark energy streamers that in those times appeared on the horizon periodically. Although all knew of the realm where a dark lord, a very noxious being, held sway over much lesser beings and continuously subjected them to his bottomless well of hate and dank thoughts, many did not realize that the corrupt mission that dark lord had chosen could and would, ultimately affect all worlds and infect as many as possible. It was as each Universe and each world within them began to rise more and more to a more perfected civilization of itself, that the demonic realm plotted its attacks against all Star Keeper races. This was prior to the Creation of the Earth Star planet. And so it was that the infernal dance began.

Yes, Children, as I stated earlier, all worlds, all Universes, have had tumultuous times and unruly Planetizens. What happened next can only be described by MySelf, as a vitally important conference with all Luminescents, all representatives of all worlds, the Creator and basically all of Divinity present. What took place at that conference affects why you are here this day. Because We had all encouraged all beings on all of Our worlds to use sentience as their manner of living and coping with life issues, it was easy for any one of them to foresee what was going to take place. All knew that if something was not done to forestall and then permanently stop invasive encounters with the primary dark lord and its lesser lords, all life forms could be destroyed and worlds lost. The Creator asked which of Us would be willing to accept the task of Creating a new world dedicated to the slow growth of the inhabitants who still needed to be chosen. There had to be a selection process in order to determine who left and who stayed on their own home worlds. It was decided that this would be accomplished through a process of culling those Souls from all other worlds who had already either showed signs of, or were already, engaging in deleterious activities. Obviously, it was not meant for them to come here without strong support from other more balanced Souls.

I could say about Myself, *"To this day however, I am a bit unclear if I actually volunteered or if it was just that no on else wanted to do it."* However that would not be true. I will only say that I accepted this mission because of certain principles of Universal Law this event was founded on.

Children, please understand how extremely important our decisions were. We were in total awareness that all plans We implemented on that auspicious day would affect all life forms **everywhere.** We also knew without a doubt in our Souls that *in time,* We would all have to confront the dark energies while painstakingly protecting all worlds. *And you think YOU have it tough!* It has always been our sense of humor that has assisted Us in dealing with the dark. In case you are curious about this, I can tell you that dark energies do not have a sense of humor. BUT they do have an intensely bitter and baleful way of deriding the LIGHT through ill-chosen words **disguised** as their version of humor.

OK, now that you are relearning what you once knew and still do know on a SuperConscious level about the *"The Great Odyssey,"* I will tell you about the "selection process" that began shortly thereafter. We all reconvened soon after that conference. Each of Us brought with Us Our carefully thought-out ideas about what this *new world to be* should have. We did so in order to support Our grand experiment of Creating a new race of beings composed of MANY races of beings. Each "new race" would have a special genus that would ultimately benefit the new world and ALL worlds. The Creator and I synchronized all of the thoughts and sentience that each representative had and merged them all with Our own. The decisions had been made and the plans were then in the process of being carried out. We Created a world of plentiful water, fertile landmasses and CLEAN air. The solar system was in a unique position that allowed it to properly induce the energies necessary to cause a consistent regeneration on the planet through seasonal "expectations." It was in this manner that all the stars, the moon and the Sun became the progenitors of new seeds. Part of their mission was to carry the seeds through the elements of nature, thereby further propagating foodstuffs for example. The Earth Star planet was Created very quickly, but if you prefer the infamous *big bang theory,* then file it next to the theory of your APE *"descendancy."*

Every Universe began a quick but thorough exploration of the actions, motivations and desires of each Soul who lived on each world. It was in this manner that it was easy to discern which Souls needed to leave the planet. The Souls who were tainted were joined by other Souls who were not. The stronger Souls were asked to accompany the weaker Souls here, so they could all learn from one another's human life experiences and begin a better race of beings rather than a tainted race of beings. They would all begin a specified period of mortal life on the planet to be called, *"the Earth Star planet."* It was also decided which mentors would sign-on to guide each Soul through mortal life. For the sake of brevity We simply at first referred to the planet as, "the schoolhouse planet." Yes, Children, in one sense it was a massive undertaking. But too much was at risk. There could not be worlds lost or defiled by the unilluminated Children. Of course it took no time at all for those beings to realize what the plans were. They knew the carefully laid out plans were for the protection of worlds and simultaneously carrying out the Creator's plan for the birth of a new world of beings. Furthermore, they knew that this new race could eventually expand their consciousness exponentially.

Ok now, I realize that what I am about to say may be confusing to some of you Children; however it needs to be said. I may only be able to simplify this explanation a bit. It will be when you leave mortality that your understanding will be clear. The human race as a collective, was birthed as individual Souls. However, it is the Creator who gave birth to the individual SOUL; yet each Soul can and does over long epochs of spatial understanding, give birth to Itself as other Souls. When the human RACES were initially Created BY the Creator, I too did assist in this process, along with the aid of the Creation processing, Star Keepers from every galaxy initially visited the Earth as the new influx of Souls arrived here and encoded NOT implanted, the genes of each Star Keeper race into the human race.

All right now, to summarize this event: the Creator and I <u>CREATED</u> the human races. However each planet, each world within each benevolent Universe, sent their respective Star Keepers to the Earth Star planet to "interact" with each of the human races. *This was accomplished through the process of seeding each race with the genetics of each planets' inhabitants AND genetically encoding each Soul with specific monitors.*

Children of Earth, your ancestors are **of** and **from** the stars. Of course I know few of you are aware of this fact. It is in complete opposition to all that your religions have taught you and in opposition to what your families and peers have also been taught and still believe. Yet it does not change the fact that it is TRUE. Our combined wishes were that each of your races here, each culture that is but a mirror image of so many other cultures on your home worlds, would be able to disassociate themselves from the blistering effects of the sociopathic unilluminated energies here and bring peace **within** each culture. Peace and understanding were and still are two of Our primary goals here. Understand now that so many of the same Souls who truly had a great need for remedial education and were here then, are still here today, wearing different forms and bearing different names. Because of their less than satisfactory Soul status on their home planets, yes, I <u>asked</u> them to come here to this planet, so that the re-education process could begin **at first** on a strictly "newbie" level. Although there have been millions of people here who have left the planet since then and traveled on to citadels of higher learning, it is still sad that so many, many, more have had to return here again and again, until such time that they acquiesce to the development process or are sent to a different plane of reality. There is a plane that had been Created solely for the Planetizens who required a one-on-one teaching method.

As all this took place then, the Star Keepers from other home worlds watched diligently over all the Earthbound Children and in accordance with the Children's pre-birth agreements, either stepped forward to protect them from harm or stepped back and allowed things to happen. No, although you may think this to be a fault on the Star Keepers' parts, I speak of their decision to NOT simply help each Soul, I did tell you they must adhere to the Soul agreements without violating any Universal Law. The Star Keepers have had to learn to do this through the painful experience of the realization that long, long, ago, they themselves were not a civilized or peaceful race or races of beings. However that having been said....there are Souls here walking in mortality whose exclusive missions are to remedy what they can and teach, teach, teach. They are a great compilation of **all** Star Keeper races, just as Earthizens themselves truly are. When necessary and when it has been predetermined that such and such a person, landmass or animal species, must be defended at all costs, the Star Keeper Warriors step forward quickly to truncate evil wherever evil's lair may be. They also use telepathy to warn individuals of incoming or impending invasive attacks that will be launched at SPECIFIC Earthbound Children.

They do this when they know that the Children they are communicating with can and WILL unhesitatingly and in quick succession defend themselves and destroy the ones who are intent on either killing them or breaking their Spirits. All the races from all other Universes constantly use the monitoring system that was devised by some of the greatest minds of all the Universes. It allows the Star Keeper forces to correctly gauge the levels of devious mind-stopping and heart- shocking plans that the dark streamers are setting into motion. This in turn shows the Universal forces how empathically each Child here is reacting to an outside stimulus. There are "stimulus factors" here hidden in plain sight, that so many of the Children do not even know exist. It also allows these forces to monitor an unusual stimulus begun by another person that MAY be intentionally transferring itself to a goodhearted Child. And of course the situation with free radicals is prominently displayed for the forces to see. In this manner they are able to gauge the damage that may be taking place and decide what needs to be done to alleviate the situation.

The greater the assaults on this planet have become, the greater the forces need to be ever ready to stimulate the Children's minds through telepathy and protect the planet as a whole. All the forces work with your Gate Keepers, your Spirit Guides and of course, your Master Teachers. Yes, the unilluminated ones, also known as *"the Illuminati,"* learned much to their chagrin as a collective body, that these Star Keepers are a force to be reckoned with. Meanwhile another fact that so many of My Children here are either unaware of or do not want to know, concerns the literally millions of Star Keepers who have been and still are, giving their very lives above your skies here, while engaged in fierce battles with the SATELLITES of the dark lords. The satellites are in some cases unmanned but have been collecting information about the planet and who is thinking what and why. Others are manned "to the teeth" with members of the ravenous entities set on conquering this planet and thus

EVENTUALLY eliminating the human races as a whole. It is because those lesser children are sociopathic that they are impervious to threats, whether the threats are veiled or blatant. They must live to kill and kill to live.

Children, when a planet or an entire Universe is placed in such a physical position that whatever destructive actions take place on that planet, can and will physically affect other solar systems and other worlds, then it must not be permitted to happen. Life is precious, so to allow any planet to be completely overtaken and destroyed is simply untenable and unthinkable. The forces are still working fervently to save whatever landmasses Terra has decided must be saved and which ones must CONTINUE to be altered. The forces' airships are visible above this world at all times. Each has a commander and is fully equipped with all of the off-world technology necessary to combat the ships of the others and also maintains a complete crew. These crews are scientists, medical personnel, Warriors and others who are necessary to provide a strong complement of male and female beings. These Planetizens are ready, willing and able to defend themselves, this planet and their own fleets. Of course it was desired that the Earthizens would rally themselves and become the long desired cohesive force We always knew they could become. In this manner it would be easier on the Star Keepers from other worlds, because they would not be so inundated with battles and the complacency on the parts of the Earth Star Children.

Do ANY of you understand the great sadness those Star Keepers feel when observing all their descendants falling more and more into the quagmire of decadence and ignorance? Think about your families, friends, peers, governments and religions that are still doing this. Does it cause you great happiness? *Hopefully not.* Yes, Celest, I will now speak of *walk-ins.* Actually I had intended to do so anyway. Walk-ins have always played an important role in the stabilization of a civilization and have a strong influence on each world. Here on the Earth Star planet they must be both "the forest and the trees." It is the way it is. Walk-ins enter in nearly all cases during a near death experience that a human has here; these are the humans who contracted with the walk-in realm and agreed to the Soul exchange. Celest and David are only a part of a small group of walk-ins who are allowed to reveal their true identities. I will not go into the reasons *at this time.* All Planetizens have the *opportunity* to function as walk-ins; once they meet a certain criteria that is. So much is predicated upon the Soul status and the true evolutionary pace that each sets for themselves, BY themselves. It is nothing that another can do for you. It is YOU and YOU.

No, walk-ins are not simply beings from only one planet, one Universe. They are from here, there and everywhere. Their sentience is vastly different from the average being here. Walk-ins also exist on many levels of "knowing." For some, it may be their first experience so YES, they do have it harder than the more experienced ones.

Just as in any life experience the first time can be a compilation of many "telling' moments. Yet, even though some of the less mature ones may fall off the path, after all they are still learning, through the process of reincarnation and the memories of their Souls' desires and intents to succeed, they ultimately relearn from all that had befallen them and start all over again. Walk-ins may choose to remain as such until a time arrives that I gently ask them to assist Me on other realms. My Celestial Blue Star Child however, is a tad more hardheaded than many others. Perhaps If I could just persuade her to stop challenging herself, she will become satisfied with all that she has succeeded in accomplishing. Even though I have gently chided her many times about this....it doesn't look too good for My ratio of success in this matter! Walk-ins, in particular the most mature Souls, use their own accrued knowledge and awesome sentience to pave their roads in mortal life a bit more carefully than do others. Some are Warriors, some are teachers or healers and some are

Warriors who are teachers as well. It is a difficult situation at best for walk-ins. They are simply not accepted as "normal" by most of My Earthbound Children.

Fortunately they all know, or are in the process of learning, not to try to fit in...because they can not. I do understand the loneliness they all experience, some more than others. However, *"When two or more are gathered in My NAME"*............. Most born-ins tend to feel awkward and a bit uneasy when encountering a walk-in for the first time. It really is a simple matter of the intellect stuck in non-recognition of an energy it can not identify. Remember please Children, when the intellect can not recognize something, can not find a "round hole for a square peg," fear then always ensues. Many walk-ins per pre-birth agreement are soldiers, sailors, marines, policemen and policewomen and so on. They place themselves in the line of battle in order to spare another person. In a real sense, they take their place knowing full well that the probability of them surviving is not high. No, not all walk-ins are in complete conscious awareness of why they do this. On a Soul level however, THEY KNOW. When it is your time, when you each arrive in Nirvana, you will understand all the reasons for this. There are things I shall **not** reveal in the current time! Walk-ins had to struggle to attain positions in governments; the same dark streamers you all contend with are always on the prowl, searching for walk-ins. Those energies destroy as many walk-ins as possible. They are always searching for the most important ones, those who are the elite. The *elite,* in this sense, are the cream of the crop. They make very, very, big targets. Understand however please, that very, very, few people who have achieved a high-ranking position in life are willing to participate in the exchange of Souls program. They would have to abandon their former life "of privilege" by allowing a walk-in substitution. Depending on the personality the walk-in is assuming, they can be graceful or clumsy, highly intelligent or of low intelligence, very motivated or not motivated at all. Yet, they still remain the staunchest of all beings that enter here in order to *serve and protect.*

The dominant walk-ins tend to gather the weaker ones and offer comradeship and re-education for the others. In this manner the evolutionary beat goes on and on. Yes, as the truly multidimensional beings they are, they can be found fighting side by side with other outstanding Warriors and teaching side by side with other prominent teachers. All at the same time when necessary. They are on and in every Universe. There are some, not too many, that do have serious problems adapting to Earth and some of the inhabitants' outlandish ideas. These are the ones who decry in the most painful emotional way, the fact that they can not simply just live only in the Spiritual world while they are on planet. Many of them choose to shorten their lifespan simply through the natural process of inner grief that is so intense that the physical vehicle simply shuts down. Each must make their own choice in this matter. Now Celest, I am going to ask you to do something for Me, just as I am asking David as well.

I ask you to please take your time now and tell the people how the Earth Star Children and their ways of life affect you. Please, speak of your experiences in such a way that it will further enlighten them about Star Keepers from other planets, and the Earthbound Children themselves. Also, what regrets you may have about your being here. This is all important Child, so I ask you to honor My request.

Celest... Well, God, of course I will honor any request from you. Its just that I was not expecting this and I am sure neither is David. This is not as simple to do, God, as it is to just be a scribe. *Their ways of life:* The citizens of Earth tend to make their lives very complex, living through logic and not even acknowledge sentience. Most really do not know HOW to live. This year, in July, marks 22 years since I walked-in here. I have seen very little change in most people. At least, not good changes. Too many people here mock what they do not understand and by that mockery cause other people to do the same. It is its own contagion I guess. This is definitely not "home." I know all walk-ins experience the same intense aloneness that David I feel. It is something that is difficult to assuage. It is when we can surround ourselves with others who are like us, or with Earth people who are ever striving upward regardless of what the personal risk is to them, that we feel such great pleasure and a very brief respite from the aloneness. People here fritter their lives away in the most degrading ways. They indulge in gossip, bigotry, prejudice and "one-upness" that I find so Soul shattering. Too many people here live their lives **through** others, instead of living their lives **through** themselves.

There is a grievous lack of respect for anyone they meet if the person they meet does not fit the mold of who they think a person should be. Too much ego, not enough Spirit. I do not like the fact that some people fear me. It would be ludicrous to me if it were not so sad. I always live without any safety net; that fact itself alarms people because they do not consider that to be "normal." My usual response to people who say that is, *"there are many degrees of normalcy and normal is only separated from your own expectations in Life when you are not living as a Soul truly should."* That is usually when they really freak out." When I am home, we all interact with great joy and spontaneous recognition as we constantly compare our knowledge with one another and further Create new ideas and new beginnings for ourselves that will take place in an upcoming incarnation.

We do not use monetary based systems, but we not merely survive, we live very well because of our own horticulture, our own clean, harmless technology and the understanding of the Soul importance of always sharing with others. Here on Earth, I have not met many people who are willing to live a more simplified but healthy lifestyle. However when I do, my heart quickens with anticipatory contentment, knowing all that those people will eventually evolve to be. It always gives me such great happiness! I have traveled to so many places here and lived in so many, many, places, without my ship of course, and every place I go I always find small quiet groups of people who truly do not only WANT change, but are willing to MAKE changes. I love these people so much. Some of them are walk-ins, some are walk-ins who do not yet know that they are, and some people are born-ins.

It does not matter a bit to me which they are; what does matter is that I know this planet needs all the help that good people can give. It is why I work as hard as I do and connect with all those I can who are now slowly moving into the "stadium" of the collective consciousness. I never wonder if these people will survive or not. I know the ones who will and the ones who will not. Many people have become desensitized here, they have lost their humanity. I am so grateful that I have seen great acts of kindness, of compassion and true courage in life and death situations performed by the people here who are **the TRUE human beings.** I have also seen the incestuous people, they have no idea that I know this about them, potential murderers and rapists and people who are hell-bent on continuing to spread terrible lies and finance anti-democracy movements all over this planet. I know some good people who are true humanitarians and although they want to be part of those who make a difference, their united voices fall on ears that can not hear. Nuns and priests tend to fear me on sight. All right, I do see humor there because they do not even know me. I have worked with some fine doctors, philanthropists and other non-fiction writers. Yet even they were voices calling out in the wilderness for a very long time. I feel such great sadness for Terra; she and I speak often about the outrageous situation she has been placed in. I speak with all the animal life forms and they love me on sight. I speak with the trees and grass and insects....not with the gnats and flies though. I have "gnat and fly issues!"

I do feel great sadness for the teenagers and young adults who do not seem to WANT to change. They would rather belong to frivolous sororities and fraternities and want "pep rally" lives. How sad. They are simply not learning, nor do they want to. *What regrets do I have?* NONE. I chose to be here in this gridline intersection. I chose to live as much as possible, as a human woman. I knew full well what I was walking into and understood with complete clarity what a difficult situation it would be. I am saddened by the fact that so many people I have worked with over the years have backslid **by their own choice,** they are now falling and I let them. Regrets? Not a one, God.

God... Thank you Celest, I could not have said it better. However, you did leave something out. Do you remember when just a few months ago while you were showering what happened and where your mind was as you were conducting your own soliloquy? I waited until you had finished berating yourself and then I spoke to you about what you had been thinking. Please share that incident with the people.

Celest... God, sometime you just do not make things too easy! David and I had been feeling very sad for days because of certain people we loved and had worked so hard with for the purpose of teaching them how to help themselves and then the great change occurred. Suddenly, these individuals just stopped trying. Even worse, their personalities changed, some of them became involved in intimate relationships with psyche vampires and of course they developed "short term memory loss." We did not know them anymore. They certainly did not know who they had been, nor were they aware that they had fallen so hard and so fast. In the shower, I was thinking about all of that and feeling so very, very, disappointed in these people. I started to wonder about myself. I do remember thinking, *"I must be crazy, I must have lost my mind. I must be a lunatic because I WANTED to come to this planet. I came here DELIBERATELY. Is what brought me here an act of lunacy or an act of God? I really must be crazy because I did this ON PURPOSE!"*

God... OK Celest, I will let you off the shower hook now. The tremendous sadness and intense disappointment with people that you experienced that day, set off a rocket to the Universe that I could not ignore. Do you remember how I spoke with you about those things that day? No, Child, I will not share that with the public. It is just too personal. Suffice it to say that I reassured you that NO, you are not a lunatic, YES in a greater sense it was "an act of God," and that you were merely overwhelmed that day by overworking and lack of sleep. Readers, let this be a lesson to you all. Do not allow your disappointment in others to cause you to feel disappointed in yourselves. That simply will not do. Now Celest, do you have any questions for Me?

Celest... God, I have only one issue I would like you to discuss. By the way though, that day in the shower....I should have known, *nobody flies under God's radar.* His radar is everywhere. My question is simply about Terra. I know this is not really a question that is too relevant to this chapter; however, I feel it should be addressed. How well does Terra adapt to the changes caused by centuries of abuse by the people and how is she coping with the changes she is now enacting here?

God... Good question Celest. OK, it had taken many millennia for My Terra Child to arrive at such a state of utter destruction that it basically made it impossible for her to continue on as she was. I have spoken in the past of the meetings I had with her to discuss her horrendous situation, so I will not state them again. Terra did not adapt to the ruthless manhandling that was thrust upon her. For a very long time however, she did try to alter certain conditions in air and topography, in the dim hope that humans would see what they were doing and realize that if she was destroyed, they themselves would also die. After a considerable stretch of linear time elapsed, it became clear to her that she could on her own, do no more.

So, when permission was granted to her for her to begin to shift herself, allowing a gravitational pull to take place and to alter landmasses, air and weather, she also gave warning of her intent and the plans she had to carry through with, to all animal, flora, fauna, all mammals in the waterways and other life forms on the planet. She then spoke with all the Overseer Spirits of each animal species and informed them of her plans. She asked that they begin the process of relocating SOME of each species so that each species would eventually evolve, even if each of them had to be temporarily displaced. She will continue on her invigorated COURSES of actions until the Jesus THE Christ Consciousness, aided by NESARA and the Winds of Change, complete their journey here and the GOLDEN NOW holds **full** sway over this planet. The NOW is already present but still must come to complete fruition. As for Terra, **she MUST play the hand she has been dealt.** *The dealer is the human race.*

Celest... God, thank you so much for all the wonderful information. I have no doubt it will benefit all who read Your words.

God... And thank you, Celestial Blue Star, for never giving up.

God *(received by David)* Well here it is the fourth of July, 2011 and unlike so many other Planetizens My beloved Celestial and David are hard at work writing My words. Their dedication to service is exemplary and I will always be beholden to them. Now, as I continue with this chapter I wish to inform those of you who are still in doubt about the accuracy/origins of My words, that it is indeed I who speak with you now. I see that much of what has been shared with you by Me is not "common knowledge" and therefore conflicts with your rational side. Do not be ashamed of this, because if you do not believe Me now, I assure you that most of you will before you leave this planet.

Evidence of My Star Keeper Children's unobtrusive presence is all around you and it is intensifying as We speak. Their sheer numbers would astound all of you, even those of you who are aware of their existence and are welcoming their help. It is not easy for them to continue to conceal themselves from you when their ultimate desire is to *help you to help yourselves.*

Their ships of light are currently being spotted all over this world; even your media can no longer completely conceal their presence. So many of you ask, "Why is it that the governments do not acknowledge the ships presence?" In simple truth some of them are the same as many of you still are, uncertain of *the E.T.'s* true intent. Therefore, they will continue to treat you as they have always done, for as long as they can, as immature *children*. Many of you still wonder, "Are there some obscure underlying reasons for their presence at this time?" "Are they really here to take control over this world and its vast resources in an attempt to hoard it all for themselves, or could they possibly be here to collect slaves to work on other colonies as is portrayed in overdramatized movies?" This is the kind of nonsense each of you who are in awareness is going to be confronted with in the days ahead. I ask you to keep a cool head, know when to speak your truths and when to hold your tongue and listen. The fear of the unknown is a powerful force.

The dominant human societal belief is that you are the only sentient life form and that you are all alone. Poppycock. If this were true why do you think so many of your scientists, astrologers and the like are so interested in exploring and controlling what you call space? If all the other planets were devoid of life forms, then what really would be the point? Yes David, it would be a big waste of SPACE. For some time now most of you have been aware of the intelligence levels of many of the animal and mammal species here on this world. Would it surprise you to know that many of these are Star Keepers themselves? Would it surprise you to know that many of My Children from other planets come here exclusively for the purpose of connecting with these beings? Why would these animal forms connect with those Star Keepers but not with you? These Star Keepers I speak of were ready to have a reunion with those animal beings, most of you are not. If the Star Children from other worlds had arrived to interact with all those who live beneath the waters and those who live on the land before it was the correct time to do so, can you imagine the chaos that would have ensued as Earthbound Children witnessed those reunions? No matter what My Star Keeper Children do, when the time comes and it will, for them to show themselves en masse for the entire world to see, there will be a panic that will spread through the hearts and minds of many people of this world. We cannot change that, we have already tried. The group populations have been too well conditioned by others. Through each of you we have been able to reach a great many other people who would not otherwise have been able to find out more about this Universe they live in and the lives of those in other Universes as well.

Each passing day brings each of you closer to reconnecting with others who are from your home worlds. Each small understanding you have also brings you closer to living as a family. Every moment that elapses brings you one step closer to the truth about why you chose or were chosen to be here now, at this pivotal time in Earth's history. Each day, despite all that you have had to endure, brings you closer to reuniting with My Self. This pleases Me greatly. Children, My arms can open quite widely and I have a very large lap, so join Me when you need to for I always have time for you. Thankfully this fallacy of the separation which supposedly exists between us will end soon. Although there is a small scattering of planets that are the lairs of the dark agents, those known as the Illuminati, they are mostly composed of those who are teetering on illusionary belief issues. We shall remove the final taint there as well. One by one, one world at a time, the cleansing goes on.

Ok, let's move on shall We? So now that you know more about the process of how the Earth Star was conceived, let Us explore some of the wondrous things My Star Keeper Children are doing on your behalf. Only vanity or ignorance would lead you to assume that they as individuals are only interested in Terra's resources to use for themselves. Also, contrary to what you may believe they look upon each of you as equals. They see no one better than another and none less important than another. Each Soul, no matter of Its current level of evolvement, is equally as important as is the next. We, none of Us, can choose one Soul over another, or We would be no better than those that seek to continue their savage hold upon this world. Many Star Keepers who are here now have experienced the Earth Star Walk themselves; they too have danced the dance of the unenlightened and flirted with a world in decay. They rose above it just as each of you will... *some* day. So many of them CAN relate to what you are going through.

These Star Keepers who are here now fight for your right to be. "To be," in this sense is your right to *freely choose* to continue to do more than just simply exist. I know that your physical concerns at the moment may outweigh your desire to connect with that higher part of you that is in communion with the entirety of Creation. Do not take this the wrong way, but... choosing to enhance your Spiritual connection, your Spiritual Self, may well be your only means of remaining connected with this world.

As I have stated many times in the past, the Star Keeper contingents are not here to do the work for you or to replace you and inhabit this world. They spend vast amounts of what you term "time" to carefully analyze each element of this world. They need to know exactly what needs to be done and how much will be required of them in order to accurately assist you in restoring fertility to all the elements of this world. Currently there is little fertility to be found. The more you do to help yourself, to help each other, the easier their jobs will be.

They and I watch as the turbulent personalities of those who are still lost in the illusion of time impacts upon those of you who are beginning to wakeup from your slumber. Some people are convincing themselves to remain in their current state as a *sleeping* being. Do not be confused, making the choice to begin the long arduous journey of moving forward is not an easy one to make, especially if a person does not know that they are in need of making the choice. You see, in order for anyone to move their center from a practical world existence to one that is Spiritually based, all they need to do is do the right thing for the right reason. It does not need to be any more complicated than that. I watch the frustration of those I have sent here to teach others of this simple concept when the ones they are trying to teach just don't seem to get it. These Star Keepers in past times, previous to the NOW times, utilized patience and persistence as an effective means to get through to these types of people. Since there is so little time left now they have had to resort to other means. What does this mean for all those who are still wavering? You will out of necessity be forced to become more independent and you must be willing to do whatever it takes to continue your lessons, alone if need be. The teachers among you, those who are both on and off world know what you do not, they have barely enough time to get their current messages out before the need has arisen to get the next ones in motion. In other words, they simply do not have time to be repetitious in their teachings any longer, you must be willing to dedicate as much time as YOU need to absorb the material and match the pace that this world has set for you to keep up with.

Throughout the many millennia many of the forces of this Universe and other Universes gathered together time and time again, to carefully scrutinize the information they had gathered together about the Illuminati forces and their designs upon this world. Through these interactions We were able to determine the best course of action to take when combating their nefarious plans. It will not be until the final bell tolls here on this world and the dark energy streamers are completely eradicated from this world, that We will be able to completely focus our attention on all the other worlds that are in need of Our service. Those of you who are on your Earth Star Walks now, those of you who will successfully complete your personal and planetary missions, will probably be called upon by Me to assist these other orbs. It IS what you do. It is what all Star Keepers do. Be aware of the fact that although there are always obstacles to every endeavor, this one you undertook here on the Earth Star, will remain prominent in the minds and hearts of all who chose to participate in the process of setting Terra free.

Throughout your remaining time here you will be observing humanity's contact with its brethren from other worlds in a manner that has never before been achieved. You see, in the past We have had limited **one on one** contact with those of you who were incarnate. **I have spoken of the necessity of this before**, what you did not know is that even during the darkest of times there was always a gathering of Star Keepers everywhere on this world whose missions were to continue protecting you from yourselves. This was not an easy task, so I ask this of you, when the Universal Doors swing wide open and the people of all nations come in contact with their respective off-worlders, please do not burden the Star Keepers with tedious, inane questions. Instead, ask them how you can be of service to them. Ultimately in this fashion you will be helping yourselves. So much of the information you need to know about how to interact with them has already been shared with you. Study it now so you are better prepared for the inevitable "next contact," not the first. The more you can steer away from the trivial questions and get to the heart of the matter, the more quickly you can begin working together to repair the damage done to this, your temporary home world. Learn to look beyond the obvious, it does not really matter which home world you are originally from, it does not matter if you were King Arthur in a previous lifetime. What does matter is who you are here in the present. Stay focused on this, please. There are mountains to move and oceans to heal before your stay here is finished. Observe these events and remember well all that you see, for it will be up to those of you who will return yet again, to help in teaching the upcoming generations.

My Star Keepers are gallantly charging into the fray on your behalf, respect them and honor them for this. No, most of you are not yet ready to engage the dark forces in one on one combat. You are going to learn though however painful it may be, that at some point in your future you may be called upon to protect whichever world you may call home at the time. Do so without fear. Never be afraid to ask for help. Do not decide to become martyrs to your cause at this late date. There is no room for theatrics in a combat zone. Your focus must remain on the task at hand. You may be wondering where I am going with all this. Let Me just say this; as Earth takes her rightful place in the Universal brotherhood and sisterhood, representatives from this world will be joining those from other worlds at the High Council meetings, to actively participate in all decisions pertaining to My Universe. I caution **all** of humanity, with this new alliance there is great responsibility. You as individual races can no longer think of Earth as a separate entity. She, all of you, are a part of something greater than yourselves. Do not make light of what I am saying to each of you. That would be a grievous mistake!

Each succeeding generation of Earthizens will be asked to take part in the Creation of new worlds. Some of you may once again call Earth your home, but it is the collective you *as a unified race of beings,* who will be venturing out into the vast *unknown* parts of space in search of new experiences, that will ultimately propel you to new heights of awareness. No longer will you be confined to choosing a human experience solely here on Earth. Does this please you? It should. Imagine all that you will learn, all that you will be able to teach others about. This alone should compel you to do your very best right now, to help this to become a reality.

David, please insert what I said to Celest in her part of this chapter.

God said, "I ask you to please take your time now and tell the people how the Earth Star Children and their ways of life affect you. Please, speak of your experiences in such a way that it will further enlighten them about Star

Keepers from other planets, and the Earthbound Children themselves. Also, what regrets you may have about your being here. This is all important Child, so I ask you to honor My request."

God...OK David, I now ask you for your own perspectives based on your experiences here.

David... I would have to start by saying that life here is certainly not dull or boring. Hmm, where does one start? I have spent a great deal of time watching and listening to those living in their familial circles. I wonder how many of them realize that they are in fact interfering in their children's destinies by not stepping back and allowing their children to make their own choices in life. I have seen grandmothers and mothers that have an insatiable desire to be completely influential in their family's lives, almost to the point of suffocation. "Do this, don't do that, grow up to BE somebody." The children are taught that they can do anything when they grow up, *as long as it adheres to their families desires for them*. They do not realize that whoever the person *grows up* to be, should be their choice. This saddens me. Families should guide the children, teach them to the best of their abilities and then let them begin their own journey. If the parenting is correctly done, everything will turn out just fine, **if** that is the individual's choice. Children grow up much too fast anymore; they are being cheated out of having **the experience of being a child**. No wonder they have a hard time remembering in adulthood that they are always to retain the essence of being "a child a heart."

I wonder how many realize that by allowing *the death of a dreamer*, they are very possibly eliminating from Earth's history the next Mozart, Picasso or Mandela. Sadly, some of God's most gifted Children are clinically diagnosed as schizophrenic, delusional or possessed. Have you ever *really* gazed into the eyes of a handicapped person and seen the Beautiful Soul inside who is just anxious to get out and share their truths? I try to imagine how it must affect God and all the Star Keepers, to watch so many people being misused, abused, killed and locked away in insane asylums simply because they were somehow different, special, or worse yet, just in the way of someone's idea of progress. I know how deeply it affects me. These are experiences I would never wish any Soul to ever have to feel. It is as if a dagger pierces the heart.

I walked in at a very young age, yet wise enough to intuitively know that war, death and destruction on any level is unacceptable. When I hear about "a casualty of war," or "acceptable levels of collateral damage," or those who do something terribly wrong and then "plead insanity," I just cringe. Are people really that naive? When I was young and knew little about plutonium and its nuclear applications, I still just knew that something about it was all wrong. The more I learned about this world, its history, humanity's vanity, its arrogance, acceptance of cruelty and most people's ability to turn a blind eye to injustices forced upon another, the more I wondered *WHY* did I choose to come here in the first place, this is in no way like the home that I came from. Of course I know why I am here, I *have* chosen a side and I AM taking a STAND for what I believe in. I realize that it may not be the most understandable choice in some people's eyes, but as Celest and I have said many times," *we are not here to win a popularity contest.....and it's a darn good thing too.*" I do not expect many people to grasp the reasons of why we do what we do, how could they? No one has ever shown them any other way to be. So we continue to do what we do best, we teach by example and through thought processing.

Another issue that disturbs me greatly, and I know that I am not the only one, is people who *need* to spend millions of dollars on first, second and even third homes, yachts or airplanes, and those that need to have six to ten thousand square foot homes when it is just one or two people living there. And let us not forget governments that spend billions on defense or paying farmers not to grow crops. Have I missed the picture here, did I get off at the wrong stop? Are there not starving, homeless, sick and uneducated people all over this planet that need our help? Couldn't this money and these resources be put to much better use, all without compromising the quality of life? I keep having the strange thought, *"like shaking the fleas off a dog's back."* I believe that is referring to what this planet was about to do with the entire human race had not The Creator, the God of this Universe, all the other Luminescents, and the unified Star Keeper forces stepped forward with their commitment to aid this dying planet.

I cannot begin to understand the shock and awe so many Star Keepers must feel when they enter into the denseness of this world. To me it would be a direct violation, an assault on their very essence, I know it is on mine and I have had ample time to learn to adapt to the murkiness that envelops this world. Sometimes I think they must look down on us and think to themselves, "if these peoples' moral compasses get any further out of control, they will never find their way back home and they may well start feeding on each other pretty soon." That is my observation, not necessarily theirs. I would like everyone reading this to take a moment, or an hour, and think about all the wonders this world has to offer, your list should be long. Think about the variations of life here, how unique and special and absolutely awe-inspiring and wonderful each is. Think about the dolphins, the whales, and the beautifully colored tropical fish. Think about the deer, the elk, the giraffe, and the tiger and so on. Then look at what we as a species have done, not only to their environments that they must depend on in order to live, but to our own environment as well that WE MUST SHARE with them. Look at what **we have done** to each other. Can you now imagine *in any sense of the word*, an evolved species from another world coming here and looking upon us as the compassionate, caring, self-proclaimed intellectuals we so blindly see ourselves to be? I speak as "we," because I consider myself part of the human race. Fortunately for us, we who are the human race, Star Keepers look beyond our faults and see the *potential* for good which exists within all of us. We could shake off the truth and ignore the obvious and consider it a temporary lapse of judgment, had this not been going on for centuries, upon centuries.

A few years back when a mother ship came to this world, a great many Star Keepers *willingly* left this ship and stayed behind to be close to their "kin" here on Earth. We have been blessed with their presence here day in and day out. Their seriousness, their spontaneously infectious humor, the wealth of knowledge they brought with them, their sage advice and their desire to be of assistance to us on all levels, physical and Spiritual, is to be admired. I for one could not imagine life without their presence or their ever attentive thoughts entering into my mind. Unlike so many, I never feel <u>completely</u> alone now, for they are with me always. This is not something that I can teach to anyone; this is something that must be experienced first hand. I smile appreciatively every time I hear from someone who has *personally* learned what it means to "*have the eyes to see* and *the ears to hear*." I know from personal experience that their continuous presence here is so beneficial for me. The people here who are using both their eyes and ears make things so much easier on those Star Keepers who are here *at our and their request.*

Do I have any regrets? Long ago when I first reunited with my beautiful (in all ways) wife Celestial, she cocked her head to the side and said to me, "you must like this look, (referring to my facial features.) I remember you having it before in some of your earlier life experiences." I LOVE this planet and will return here often, if permitted. No, I have no regrets, nor would I wish to ever "turn back time." How's that God?

God... David, I think you clearly expressed in very few words what I have been trying to say for a very, very long time to My Children of this world. I thank you for your dedication to Spirit. Now, any questions for Me?

David... Were there any Star Keepers from other worlds that were invited to have a physical experience here on Earth who declined the offer?

God... Not everyone was asked, those that were asked jumped at the chance to *test their mettle.* There are many reasons why some chose not to come here, some are not yet ready, some are not finished with other pursuits, and others **choose** not leave the higher realms. David, I see the underlying thought in the back of your mind and yes, there were a great number of Souls, who wished to be here NOW for this *"God production,"* who for one reason or another were not chosen to participate in this timeline. They will all get their chances now that We are all *assured by* **Terra** that she will be around for a long, long, time to come.

David... I am sure many people here are curious about how much time it takes to get from here, well, to anywhere. Any comments?

God... Let Me use these two scribes as an example. Celest and David go to sleep at night, they journey to their *nighttime* destination, they may go home to be with their families or to a High Council meeting, or spending time with Souls in Nirvana, or wherever. They are back in their bodies before they awaken. Does that answer the question that some people may have?

David... Yes.

David... Is there any Universe that is more evolved than another?

God... I wouldn't say more evolved in the human sense of the term, certainly some are older than others, but as I have told you in the past, age does not equate to levels of evolvement. There are Universes that house civilizations that are primarily composed of very evolved Souls. In this most literal sense of the term *evolvement,* the civilizations can be more evolved even if the planet or Universe itself is considered to be young or pre-adult. There are those who are considered to be **old Souls** that are in many ways *less* mature than some of the newer Souls. I would like to add that the intent of any Universe as well as its respective Caretaker is to keep every aspect of itself in constant change, after all.... The only CONSTANT in any Universe IS change.

David... God, one more thing. You cannot imagine my disappointment when I realized that all the "Walk-ins Welcome" signs were not put there just for us.

God... Who said they weren't? I told you I would put out the welcome mat for all who were brave enough to accept My Earth Star challenge and as always, I *will* leave a candle burning in the window until you find your way back home.

God Talk 12

The Arrival of the Masters

God (received by Celest) I have on occasion spoken about highly evolved Souls who are androgynous beings; many of them are Avatars as well. I have also explained that all life forms here and on all other planets have Guardian Spirits. For instance, there is the Spirit of the Wolf, the Spirit of the cat and so forth. Each of these Spirits is the main Caretaker or OverSeer **of** a particular species of life. So it should not be a surprise to you that each race of My human Children here also have a main OverSeer, apart from Myself. At least I hope this is not a surprise to you; for if it is, then this is showing you how much you lack in Spiritual knowledge! OK, it was when the Creation Processing working in unison with MySelf, the Creator and all of the representatives from each planet, each Universe, planned our protection for the Earthbound Children, that certain agreements were conceived. It was decided upon by all that because of the vast diversity of cultures, races, and levels of Soul maturity, that it would be a good idea if specific Souls who had long ago achieved an elevated state of infinite wisdom and were incomparable teachers should be the ones to not only watch over the Earthbound races, but to protect them, and teach them.

They were to learn of the greater values and the advanced sequential steps necessary to further evolve, if they wanted to. These teachers would also assist Terra in her selections of "who stays and who leaves."

No, there was absolutely no "class distinction" that would be made here in order to separate the wheat from the chaff. All hinged on the behavior modifications, the personal and planetary intent of each Child here and the willingness, or conversely the lack of enthusiasm, of each individual to truly work for the greater good. These Souls would be required to give as well as to live as their personal best, regardless of what traumatic experiences they would encounter as a result of their own selfless efforts. Because these special androgynous beings had been Created as individual members of specific races on other worlds, they had the inherent knowledge necessary to not only relate to a race's conundrums here on this planet, but they were also in complete control of their own individual energetic mass of thought patterns and would remain passionately detached. They would not form any judgment calls against their races here on Earth, even though their races were in turmoil. All races while here on the planet have interbred with other different races, when they were on their original home planets, many, many, of them have in fact formed intimate loving relationships with other life forms from other planets. On planets where the inhabitants are asexual, there are still other means of producing offspring. In other words, one who is from Andromeda may have an intimate relationship with one who is a Venusian. So their offspring would be of mixed heritage. BUT the parent, whose lineage had a higher ratio of one ancestral race rather than several, would have less mixed heritage and would give the Child the more prominent genealogy through the rite of birth. So, if the parent who was Andromedan had more dominant race genes than the parent who was Venusian had of the Venusian race's genes, then the Child would consider himself, or be considered by others, as Andromedan. For example David is Arcturian, yet he also has Pleiadian genes. His Arcturian genes are his more dominant ones though. OK, now that I have provided you with a brief refresher course, I will continue with the Masters.

Each Master is a product of himself. Although they may wear the guise of male of female depending on which appearance or gender suits the situation better, ultimately their androgynous state shines through their entire being and literality illuminates the complete figure. I said, "a product of himself," as a way of pointing out to you that perhaps you needed a reminder of what I said in a previous time, **"all Souls birth themselves _of_ themselves."** The

Masters constantly watch over many, many, Universes. Here on the Earth Star planet they arrive periodically in response to either My asking them to be here or **by you, yourselves, calling in the Masters.** It has always been during times of great strife taking place here or on other worlds, that their help is simply invaluable. OK, when that long ago period had developed, the time when We spoke with them about certain gridline intersections that simply must take place here, we jointly agreed that there would be SPECIFIC teachers here, some of whom are walk-ins, who would unite their voices and issue the call. The teachers I am speaking of were told well in advance of their arrival on Earth in this lifetime when to call and **when** to expect "a reply." The Masters can and do work to alleviate certain conditions not only through their teaching, but also by correctly gauging the totality of delusional situations taking place involving clusters of individuals who have fallen under the spell of the uninformed. They must work to establish "damage control." They also work with those who have been religiously indoctrinated in believing many, many, lies.

Although this is but a small part of their teaching methods, each Master works with each of his Earthbound races here in an attempt to help them to see the truth. It does not mean that a Master of the Oriental race can not or will not help those of the Italian races however. Remember please, that because all races here are of such mixed bloodlines that regardless of how many Masters work with the dominant genetic lineage of a culture, they each can and do work with other races and other civilizations as well. In many instances the huge groups of people here that the Masters work with are the people who are already fulfilling their own contracts. The contracts are the "letters of intent" that had been written under the auspices of all Universal Laws. These Souls contracted to allow the Masters to work with them when they signed an agreement prior to their arrival to this present lifetime. They asked that the Masters assist them in all pivotal matters, particularly planetary events and issues. This assistance would continue until such time the Masters' help is either not needed or not wanted. Celest, I will speak more of this later, however I now welcome the entrance of *"Master Kato."*

Master Kato...Celestial just said," Well, Kato, "you're on." I thank each Soul here for inviting us to assist you in this, the greatest time for need and change. Receiving messages from any of us is not always very easy at first. Our energy levels are so dynamically well-defined that there are times when anyone walking in human form, yes, of course this applies to walk-ins as well, feel almost overwhelmed with a sense of Lightness that causes them to feel more off planet than on planet. I see Celestial will have many typos to correct as a result of this! I have been asked to speak on behalf of all of us who are the Masters. Quite obviously it is simply an impossibility for each of us to individually participate here in the *"God Forum."* So in our effort to simplify everything while providing your races with information from us as a collective, *I speak for all.* We each have a certain protocol that must be attended to. This applies to everything of **primary** importance here on the planet and to every life situation as well. We have been repeatedly called in by some very good Souls here on Earth. Yes, the God of this Universe requested our help, but that does not in any way preclude the fact that far more importantly than God calling us in, is the fact that many of you here have.

God briefly touched upon certain sequences of events that define the advent of our arrival and why. We always are informed well in advance by whoever the Luminescent in need may be, of the probability of when and where our service will be required. When it is foreseen as the most appropriate action to take, we are shown images and histories that are relevant to our participating in **the great cause.** We understand why it would be difficult for you to understand our Universal techniques that incorporate "a knowing through sentience, through Soul Voice and unity of the continuum of Soul mind." Also this includes what you would probably consider to be a type of clairvoyance, as a foolproof manner in correctly ascertaining all that needs to be altered. This manner of studying situations clearly defines how and why these problematic states of affairs occurred in the first place. This also provides us with the knowledge of which Souls we can depend on when we arrive on whatever world or worlds are under duress. If I were not concerned that I would confuse you I would explain the process. However, you can remember once you are "home." On this world though, we had long observed all the shenanigans and outright mayhem that has taken place here, seemingly since forever. We of course are an integrated part of the NOW. This is true of all sentient beings on other worlds and in other realms. So it is that everything we know through "disclosure" as well as through our observations of what is happening here and what *will* happen globally is of primary importance. All that will transpire in <u>whatever future you each have left here</u>, remains as part of our mission that requires that we further separate the changelings from the changing Souls.

We are called "the Masters," because that is who we are. No, my statement is not a parody derived from a very bad movie. We are evolved beings; we have capabilities that few others have and we always use them for the greater cause. It really does not matter if the people on this planet knew about us consciously or not. At least it did not matter until now, that is. It does not affect the reality that we are who we are and that we are as real as you are. Long ago, so far back in spatial timing that few can remember, except perhaps the Luminescents themselves, we followed a Universally dedicated program. It was achievement through right action. This encompassed learning everything that needed to be learned through a copious and conspicuous understanding that was and always will continue to be, a vitally important matrix of our individual Souls. This matrix I speak of conjoined with all other magnetically charged evolved Souls who were like us. The matrix formed a comprehensive and highly suitable force of magnetic coils and electromagnetic interaction. This movement was motivated through cause and effect, thereby birthing exchanges through the Soul and luminescence. What this essentially means is that although we are pure Light BEINGS, we can and do have the quintessence necessary to function as both teachers and "gatherers of Souls." Although we each HAVE specific expertise in all areas concerned with life, we also share our expertise through a system of combining our LIGHT FORCE in order to emanate Light as it truly is. In this manner we can overcome any obstacles or, hurdles, if you prefer that term, that are tentatively set up against us by the opposing forces. We can then diminish or destroy those obstacles at will.

The reason the Luminescent of this Universe made a point of stating that He had called us in, is to show you each that yes, He can do this. However, it is more providentially important to have the merging of the Earthbound Children's voices raised in joy and asking for our assistance, rather than have them asking when the Souls here are in such distress. *Happiness moves mountains faster than does sadness.* I have moved many a mountain range myself. Several years ago, one of our greatest combined joys came about as certain groups such as, *"the Messengers,"* who speak regularly with their vessel, our beloved Shamaan Eagle, joined voices with Celestial and David and began speaking publically about the ultra importance and absolute necessity of **calling in the Masters.** We understood then and of course we still do, how difficult a project this was for them to undertake; how difficult it is to reach out and connect with Earthbound races who have long ago forgotten our very existence. These three beloved Souls had written into their contracts that yes, they would unhesitatingly call us **when the correct gridline intersection arrived.**

It HAS arrived! Although these three beautiful ones have been connected for so very, very, long, much longer than they have known one another in this present lifetime, they each understood without questioning the matter that it was no "coincidence" that they would once again unite here and now. Shamaan and her evolved group known most familiarly as, *"the Messengers,"* have been reaching out to people to speak on our behalf about the absolute necessity of people changing before *the changing of the guard* takes place. Celestial and David have been teaching other people about us as well. However, beginning in earnest in 2009, Celestial and David began calling us in daily; many times several times a day or night. The more Celestial and David called out to us, the more we, as a collective, smiled at their obviously one-minded Spiritual stance. Of course we responded just as we did with Shamaan. It is not as though these three would have taken "no" for an answer anyway! Celestial, I will ask you to please recall some of the fortuitous meetings we held with you in response to your heartfelt and exhausted beckoning to us. Except for my own name, we would prefer that you not name any of the other Masters, please.

Celest... All right Master Kato; there have been so many, many meetings that I have had with so many Masters that it is not an easy task to recall each one of them. However, I will simply speak of some of them that I have found so endearing. The Masters immediately began responding to my calls. It began in 2009 and is of course still an ongoing event. Many beams of pure bright white Light would suddenly appear as if they were signaling me to say, *"copy that."* Then in what seemed to me to be no time at all, the Masters would appear to me, sometimes singly, other times in twos and still other times in the hundreds. I was so touched by how they each approached me. I felt so honored, not humbled, but highly honored. They each made it a point to always say, "Celestial, we are ONE." I was shown very clearly which Masters were the OverSeers of which races. In one instance two Masters, obviously very ancient beings, smiled at me after a "conversation" we had and proceeded to pass <u>through</u> the closed and locked doors. There was exquisite humor here because as they did this, the human forms they had donned no doubt to protect my eyes from the extremely bright luminescence they are composed of, remained on the main torsos of their bodies, but as they passed through the doors facing the outside, their hands and heads became extraordinary large bright balls of the purest white glowing

Light. I must say, they certainly have their own unique way of "signing off!"

Several times I have been invited to join **all** the Masters from this Universe as well as those Masters from many others. We joined together in great halls that held thousands of the Masters. We laughed and I felt so uplifted and in a strange sense, "untouchable." I knew that where I was and all those Masters I was with, were protecting me from any invasive attacks that could have been launched against me by dark forces that did not want me to be there. We stayed there enjoying one another's company for a very long time; although there are other times when we meet in smaller groups. Both "genders" were there in the great halls and were also present in the other meetings as well. Each of them wore the most beatific and most serene expressions on their faces. As God would no doubt say, "their countenance was surreal yet extraordinary." Those are just a couple of examples of my meetings with them as a collective. However, it was you Master Kato, who not only asked me to sketch a picture of you, but you gave me the correct spelling of your name. I know on Soul level, that we....the collective....have been together for as long *as I have been.* My meetings with all of you are on the same level as my daily and nightly meetings with Star Keepers from other Universes. Many of the Star Keepers have been here with me since they disembarked from the mother ship in 2007. They have said they will remain on Earth until the last bell tolls.

Master Kato... Thank you Celestial, I encouraged you to speak a bit about this because we would like all races here to become used to our continued presence here. Star Child, do not be concerned about whether everyone will believe what you just said or not. Just be happy about the fact that many people will. Others will soon be connected to us in the same manner that you are as well. People of planet Earth; let me be very clear about this, we are **not** here to save you from yourselves. That is not our responsibility. We are here to connect with the minds, hearts and Spirits of our races and in so doing, assist people in elevating themselves through the process of *changing* themselves! We are also protecting certain people from physical harm and outright death that would occur at the hands of the waning dark forces. We work with all other Star Keepers from all Universes in this matter. People on this planet who are too fainthearted and unwilling, or feel they are unable to accept the fact that this beloved Terra of the Universe will easily and without remorse continue on her journey with or without them, are the people of each race that we can not help. We, along with all the clusters of Spirit Guides and Master Teachers, deal with the priorities of who needs the greatest amount of help, what type of aid is needed and how receptive the people will be to the help.

We are currently appearing wearing human form when need be; otherwise we can be seen as we truly are. Collectively, while monitoring the conditions of the shifting topography, we are also working with the Star Keeper forces to alleviate as much of the devastating effects of the chemtrails spraying as we can without directly intervening. We are very diligently studying every landmass and waterway to see what we can effectively assist Terra with, as she proceeds with her plan of reconstituting all aspects of this Earth Star planet. It is through her ability to change the form and structure of herself that will cause further alignments of Earth working in conjunction with this solar system and provide a lush, healthy, fertile environment here, _in the centuries to come_. It can be a bit of a complicated process at times. So many needs must be taken into consideration in order for all new growth to become properly fertile and in direct alignment with the preplanned areas of both land and water where "new" more evolved animal, flora and fauna life forms will live and thrive. Yes, we have the benefit of using our advanced technology here to help us; however the new Earth movements MUST take place and be IN PLACE while the former worn-out and abused areas are displaced. Any GOOD farmer on Earth knows that when planting new fields, there are specific precautions that must be taken so that the unhealthy does not contaminate the newly planted and EVENTUALLY thriving fields. No, we do not simply tweak our noses and "make" things happen. That is very unrealistic! Yes, in one sense we too are Star Keepers; we are simply more advanced than our other brothers and sisters. In time, each will have the opportunity to become Masters, if that is what they want. As for now, as a collective we think of them as, *"Masters in training."*

I want to show you all a clear example of what is now taking place here with the issue of the waning of the dark forces. I intentionally showed Celestial a long-awaited event currently taking place because I wanted her to describe this herself, for the further edification of all people here. Celestial, please describe in detail what you witnessed.

Celest... On July 2, 2011, I was shown a HUGE picture of what I knew to be the intentional observation the Masters wanted to share with me. Other than telling David about it, I have not spoken to anyone else about this. I knew by intuiting the situation that I was not <u>at that time</u>, meant to speak of this matter. I am trying to think of the most basic way to explain what I saw, but to do so in such a manner that even the most hardened cynics would pause and reconsider what they THINK they know. I was lifted above the Earth, but at the same time I was so very close to the Earth that I had the advantage of quietly watching the entire globe. EVERYWHERE on the planet were the most enormous *craters*, I will call them that for lack of a better term, that were so deep that I wondered how they could extend so far into the Earth without touching the Earth's core. They were all cylindrical and circular shaped. The insides of each were soft, fresh, brown dirt. As l looked at the soil I saw very, very, long, extremely spindly roots. The roots had somehow been dug up and out of the base of the craters. The parts of the root systems that were dangling, "by a thread," on the loosened soil were the most unhealthy, diseased looking roots you could image. Think about plants that you may have had that were infected by a diseased plant.

When you empty out the flower pot or the plant bed, what you see there is the same thing as I am describing that I saw in the craters. I knew without being told by the Masters what I was seeing. All of the Divine forces have been working so earnestly to **uproot** the unhealthy, evil, dark that has been present here on the planet. I will ask Master Kato to continue from this point.

Master Kato... Thank you Star Child; yes, you are absolutely correct in your assessment of the situation. We decided that you should be the one to witness the event. So, you did! Earth Star races, it is important that you understand that what Celestial saw is continuing to take place even as I speak. All diseases must be cured only after the **cause** is correctly determined. Then and only then, can the healing **effect** take place. This part of the reformation process will soon be at an end. HOWEVER, during this interim, slightly before the end is revealed, all other reconstitution considerations must take place. So, as each root that has been "upturned" is exposed to the environment that removes its toxic life, the new and healthy systems are carefully being installed or set in place, for *the new gardeners to care for.* Anyone who reads our words here and considers what we are saying as, "farfetched," is already sealing their fate. I will be discussing physical "anomalies" taking place that so many of you are experiencing during Celestial's question phase, which will begin now.

Celest... Master Kato, you sort of just slipped me in here but yes, I will ask my questions now. You spoke of the anomalies taking place. Please explain that and define what levels you are speaking of, is it strictly physical, what about emotional, Spiritual or ethereal?

Master Kato... I used the term "anomalies" simply to make a point. My point is that just because people here are loath to acknowledge what are actually natural occurrences, they seem to rely heavily on seeing situations as anomalous, rather than the reality of the event. It is as we respond to the Souls here who call out to us, those who call out only in just cause that is, that we not merely align with these Souls, the more readily they accept us into their lives the more the physical vehicle itself must alter. Remember, I did tell all of you that we are pure Light BEINGS. As such, everyone and everything we align with alters in a coordination of Light Matter coalescing with lesser or Greater Light matter. So it is that those of you here who possess greater amounts of Light will feel our presence in a slightly different variation from those who possess lesser amounts of Light. If you bear in mind that the amounts of Light you each have is predicated upon you yourselves as SOUL VOICE and individual SOUL LIGHT, then it should not be difficult for you to understand this situation. Those of lesser Light usually simply lack the maturity required before they can follow the next sequential steps for amassing more Light.

Just because these are the ones who have smaller portions of Light does not in any manner define them as "dark or evil." Although we are asking each Soul here to call us in, we are going to give you a brief description of what takes place when you admit us into your lives. I said, "brief," because there are some things we would rather you found out for yourselves. Here are some of the basics: Light attracts Light. So it is that when your own Light Self conjoins with us, we who have far greater amounts of Light that are not on the same levels as all of yours, certain bodily changes occur because they must. Try to understand please, Light always valiantly struggles when it must, or flows swiftly and gently when it can, to engage other Light particles as a means of expanding itself. Worlds and Universes are built, Created, on Light. Someday you will fully understand this statement. It is as our own Light Selves arrive and join with other Souls regardless of the amounts of Light they may have individually; that the not so subtle interaction occurs of Soul touching Soul in the most beautiful arrangement of Light Matter. From the very moment it begins, the combination of Light particles become an amalgamated force that continuously births more Light because it is the nature of Light to do this. The more progressive mature Light particles ultimately strengthen the lesser Light particles and so the eternal dance of the Light correspondingly becomes an absolutely massive energy. Obviously I am not in any manner referring to the disproportionately displaced amounts of dark light that permeates those who dance with the lesser god.

The more receptive a Soul is to our combined union is the defining factor that enables the physical vehicle to alter itself in order to safely initiate the new changes. This is accomplished while alarming the intellect as seldom as possible. As a Soul progressives and shares our movement in tandem, then the physical vehicle begins the Light alteration process. Although this usually occurs at a slow pace, we have taken notice of many people here who have Super Consciously accelerated this process. The combination of our own Light that is being shared as part of a reciprocal relationship with each responding person here, causes the physical vehicle to seek to gather more Light within each part of itself. What happens at this stage is purely a natural event. Light enters into the cellular structure; at that point the Light Matter enters into each and every cell within the human body. Normally, this would occur with one cell at a time. However, much depends on the Soul's determination to allow the bodily changes to take place and at what pace. Therefore, those who have the greater amount of Light already, are more than capable of handling the upsurge of even vaster amounts of Light Matter, than for instance those whose proportion of Light already possessed is smaller.

Physical vehicles always react positively, not adversely to this noninvasive entrance of the Light. Of course there are certain striations or patterns of physical and emotional changes that result as more and more Light Matter is assimilated. All organs within the body change a bit. They can become healthier if there is not a health situation that is already preparing to cause termination to the person. Most experience a slower heart rate, for the heart no longer needs to beat faster as it once did, in order to compensate for other strains placed upon the body. The outer skin will eventually begin to feel tingly as the skin that shields the body changes itself to a clearer, more defined version of the health of itself. Most individuals experience quirky unexplainable itches, or small aches and pains as the physical vehicles insist on *gliding on the Light*. Hearing may become very acute; sometimes to the point of people feeling that all noise is distorted. Many people will also find that they will hear the most minute sounds, but to them the sounds will seem to be amplified. Some say that their vision alters; they see things in a clearer and sharper manner. Others will find out, if they do not already know, that sunlight may feel as if it has become an unusually glaring hot object. Bodies will require different amounts of food although you must learn to listen to what your bodies want to eat and what they do not want to eat. This is vitally important. Some people will find that they require either more salt or more sugar as their bodies continue to change and realign themselves. Many find themselves needing to drink more quantities of water than they had previously. At times any individual will begin to feel as though they are 10 foot tall. Body weight alters as the body itself tends to shed unwanted and now unneeded weight. This is weight that it felt it once needed in order to sustain itself. Eyes themselves have been known to change their color or their sheen. Many people complain that from time to time their hair hurts. Throughout this entire process and until such time that the physical vehicle has assimilated all the Light Matter possible, the receivers will undergo bouts of tiredness. This is all perfectly natural.

Emotionally, the mind responds to the changes at times by causing the receivers to feel as though they are on a roller coaster. This is due to the complexity of the mind itself sorting out what is natural and what is not. Soul always sets up an endless stream of reassuring messages that Soul transmits to the mind. This in turn eventually gives the mind, no pun intended, the peace of mind that it requires. As a Spiritual echelon, Soul experiences the greatest, most intense responses to all this on a conscious and Super Conscious level. It is difficult to properly express to you the exact sensations Soul has during these "opening of the Sacred doors and Channels." There simply are not any adequate words in human language that we can express. I can tell you that sentience simply explodes in sheer Light Matter and conscious understanding of the truly wondrous events taking place. In other words however, the willing participants in these momentous occasions have rebirthed themselves and are now truly willing and able to work with us, as we continue on our quest for equal just cause and Soul to Soul reconciliation. Those who are with us now and those who will shortly join our gathering are easy for you to see. They are the ones whose eyes are all aglow with the infinite brilliance of the love of God shining through.

So, this is who we are and just a bit of information about what we do.

Celest... Master Kato, no doubt there are many questions I could ask. However, personally I believe that you have shared a wealth of important information with people that will require time for them to assimilate. So with this comment to you, I thank you for all that you do as individuals and as the collective and I will leave the questions to those people here who *issue the call.* I do want to address the readers though; there are rules that are applicable when calling in the Masters. I am taking the time to let you know what they are so please, pay attention.

1.   Formulate your thoughts carefully. Determine what it is that you want the Masters to assist with. Be expansive in your thinking BUT remember they will not respond if the people calling them are strictly "service to self" people. Do not ask for "peace on Earth." If that is one of your desires then first determine for yourself how this can come about and what is the best way YOU can help in that matter. Then state that desire with the necessary information that will define what that means to you and do not ask for a timeline for that to take place.

2.   Yes, if there is help you want from them of a personal nature they will respond to your needs, HOWEVER, if you are calling them **only** for yourself do not be surprised if they do not reply.

3.   Be relaxed and do not feel intimidated when you begin to call them. They are here to help, not harm! Quiet your mind as much as possible and call them anytime you want to. You could simply state," I am calling in the benevolent Masters of the Universe." They will appear to you...when they appear to you! Oftentimes the Masters will begin communication with people while the people are in either a sleep state or a meditative state. However, they very easily and joyfully enter when a person is completely conscious as well.

4.   Always thank the Masters for all that they do. Even if you may not see signs of events taking place that you have asked for, that is only because you can not see all that is actually occurring under the Universal Law of cause *and effect*. These are my heartfelt suggestions to all of you. May you succeed in this mission with the understanding that all of you who do this, are assisting God and the Creator, in building a whole new world here **on** THIS world. Thank you for listening.

God... As always Master Kato, you and the rest of the collective have performed superbly in presenting your information. Children of Earth; now is the time for you all to begin to shout! Depending on what the situations around you are, shout out loud when possible or shout nonverbally and send your combined thoughts of joy, enthusiasm and happiness up to the Universe. You do this not only because you can, but most importantly to show that nothing and no-thing taking place here can or will, sway you from following your beliefs. Maintain the understanding that contrary to how it may appear to you to be at times, all that is taking place here is in direct correlation with what you have AS a collective consciousness, asked for. In this manner My beloved Children, you shall glide on the Light, thus preventing the dark from finding or creating any more opportunities to savage this planet. No longer shall you fall for the thinly disguised winsome ways they had used to debilitate the hearts, minds and Spirits of **you who are the pioneers of the Golden Now**. Children, each time you allow yourselves to soar to the heavenly ethers while sending your thoughts and voices to the greater "upward bound," rather than to the "Earthbound," every tiny speck of your own awesome Light forges a massive glow. This glow is a gigantic energetic orb of love. I know this is not always an easy task to fulfill. It is sometimes difficult to concentrate on doing this when your stomachs are hungry and your minds are in distress. However, I have known you each and all for as long as you have been. Trust Me when I say, "*I know far better than you do what you are capable of Creating.*" I see and hear each of you in every nanosecond of your life. I see the glory of God, the magnificence of the Creator and the indefatigable Spirit of your individual and collective Souls.

Dance Children, dance and sway to the music of the undefeated Universe. Glide your way to the tones of the spheres and laugh with your teachers and guides and the Masters every chance you have. Laughter is a great healer and a banisher of the dark. Think of some of the erroneous beliefs you once had and laugh at yourself because you had them. Those beliefs you each had back then, have in a peculiar way brought you to the threshold of personal and planetary freedom. I see the love shine in your eyes as you each arrive at the realization that, **"God is not wrong about these things."** Enjoy experiencing **loveable** tremulous sensations as you each enter into your new Light body. Children, enjoy the pleasures of the unrestricted freedom of BEING that long has been denied you. Join Me in the "circle dance;" the dance of non-constraint that is the continuation of all your new beginnings. Indulge yourselves Children, indulge yourselves in laughter, harmony and *"good conversation with all those who love you best."* Join Me in the continuum of yourselves. I await you there with great joy and greater pride in all that you are achieving. This is especially endearing to Me since so many of you are unaware that you ARE succeeding. *Glide on Children, glide on.*

Celest... God, I am not going to ask you any questions. You have stated so many important facts for everyone to learn from. After all that you and Master Kato have shared with us, any questions from me would be superfluous.

God... Thank you Celest, I understand.

God *(received by David)* The arrival of the Masters is a pivotal time in Earth's history. You may compare it's importance to the times of your first space flight, the landing of Columbus in the new world or the invention of the light bulb. Each was significant in bringing to this world a time of massive change. This timely advent of the Masters is of equal importance to all of you just as it is to this entire Universe. When working with the Masters you must always remember that they are no different than you in one regard, their purpose is to help fulfill Earth's and humanity's destinies. You may want to sit down for a while and decide for yourself just how important this lifetime is to you. The decisions you must now make are the most important decisions of ANY of your lifetimes. Once you come to the conclusion that this lifetime **really is** the most important one and that you are going to give your all to assisting the human species out of the dark ages, then and only then, should you call upon the Masters for help and guidance. You see, they have many responsibilities, so to waste their time with insignificant gestures will not be tolerated.

They can see through the illusions and delusions people have hidden away in the secret compartments of their mind. Make no mistake; they are here to walk side by side with you through all that lies before you. They will even carry you when necessary. By the time these planetary changes are over, when the Earth has finished reformatting her continental structuring, you will be long gone from mortality. But the Masters will still be here teaching all the upcoming generations of humans. For now, honor them as you would any good teacher. Listen, be attentive, ask questions, but do not interrupt them when they are sharing their sage advice with you. I mention all this because I understand the tendency of most humans to jump into situations without taking the appropriate amount of time necessary to correctly understand the information being presented to them. Understand what is being said first, and then you may formulate a response. Please respect them; they have come a long way, they have given up other important missions to be here now. Please, have no doubt about this. Now, while the Masters are here you will learn to be aware of the changes they are initiating on your behalf and by your request. Help them to help you by using the sentience you all possess. No, it will not always be easy to find the strength to endure the up and down periods and, the inevitable expressions of despair in others may set you off balance. Find a way, whatever it takes to rise above your physical vehicle if only for a minute. Hum a song, take a succession of deep breaths, loosen your mind and enter into that place where all is peaceful, quiet, calm and so serene. This is where you will do Us all the most good. The Masters can reach you here, in your Sacred spot. I realize that some of this is a little off topic, but I want you to know that it is important that you be in the right place, in the correct frame of mind, when the Masters come to work with you.

Why would the Masters choose this life of service? They are capable of doing anything "of service" they choose. I have told you before that a Soul's progression throughout eternity is based upon Its prior achievements, as well as all that It still wants to either accomplish or experience, as a means of testing ItSelf. Can you imagine a better teaching tool for yourself? Of course there is also the option of looking into the minds and hearts of those not as evolved and assist them in raising their senses to a higher plateau. The human species is a great challenge for the Masters because of the "great divide" that exists here that does not necessarily exist anywhere else throughout the cosmos. Remember well their dedication to Heavenly pursuits. There will never be a time when the Masters are not needed. Many of you will eventually join their ranks. Put yourself into their unenviable or enviable position whichever the case may be, for just a moment. Give yourself a taste of what it means to be responsible for presenting the right information at the right time in the correct sequence. Very few can formulate their thoughts that well. It is the sign of inner *knowing*. It is achieved through practice and patience. Patience is one of your tasks for this lifetime; learn it well and you will gain much. "Much" in this sense is the ability to listen. Listening and hearing are two different things, so you better understand which one you are doing. If you are among those that have not learned to practice patience and still believe that all of the changes desired for this world will be put into place over night, then you **will be** sorely disappointed and unable to function in a Light body.

The Masters have always been involved in the Earth Star processing of her students. I can honestly say that there has not been one case of a Soul graduating from the Earth Star Walk who has not interacted with these remarkable beings. To think that you could figure out everything without their input would be ludicrous. I will give you an example you can easily understand: let's say you did graduate without ever having a *conscious* interaction with the masters. I can guarantee you that somewhere throughout your journeys you have read something, or were influenced by someone who was influenced by them. Everything that has ever happened to each of you has happened for a reason. Be mindful of this fact, this fact like patience, are tools of your trade. "Trade" is *remembering* that you are Spiritual Beings having a mortal experience. Once you have reunited with your Spiritual self everything else is a walk in the park. Now, Master Kato, do you have anything to say?

Kato... Yes, God, I do. Greetings David, we have not spoken before so this is my introduction to you. You and Celestial have been calling Us in for some time now, you have each asked us to assist you in your many endeavors. These were requests that we wholeheartedly answered. To those who do not know all that these two are doing in your behalf, let me just say that they have freed more trapped Souls, dislodged greater spaces of negativity and yes, fought the beast in its own lair more times than you can possibly ever imagine. Their dedication to performance above and beyond the call of duty is a credit to themselves and their respective races, the Pleiadian and Arcturians. They are among the many from their home worlds that chose to be here now. They did not choose to enter when times were better, nor did they choose to come in after the Shift Hit the Fan and all the wrongs of this world had been set right again. No, they did as they have always done during their many incarnations here, they chose to be here in the thick of it all when their presence could do the most good.

We have watched these two, who are Masters themselves; blow the Golden Conch for all to hear. What few realize is that these two have been instrumental more than once in giving ordinary Earthizens a breather from the invasive assaults that captivated them. They did so by holding the dark forces at bay. We applaud them, this world knows how fortunate she is to have them here and now, thanks to all the people they have touched during their travels, more Souls all over this globe are finding David and Celestial and *remembering* from these two's teachings. Now, so I am not neglecting an important piece of this puzzle, let me say in our own behalf that when they **issued the call** we were here side by side with them during these God inspired projects initiated on everyone's behalf. It is a wondrous sight to behold when a person is able to lift themselves out of their physical presence and quite literally become as large or larger than life. David and Celestial know what we have all been trying to teach all of you who are reading this; there are NO Limitations to what you can achieve. This can only happen if your heart is true and your focus is trained on a single cohesive thought, rather than ones that are scattered and fractured. Use what God has given you and become the ones you have been looking for.

It is time for you to define your goals and aspirations. Define what it is that you will allow in your life and what you will not. Take a stand for those who are too weak to stand on their own, defend the principles you adhere to. Let no one come between you and the one you wish to become. Enjoy your life, be happy, not sad. Never turn the other cheek, do not associate with those who would hold you back. Learn to walk away from those who relish their sorrow. Gather yourselves together and collectively, we will align with your cause. Be true to yourself, for others will follow your truths. Be willing to walk the front lines when the horn has been sounded. Hear us when we enter your realm, for truly we do not have a minute to waste. We are waiting. Yes David, *"knock three times on the ceiling if you want me"* works for us. Till we meet again, this is Kato speaking on behalf of all of us who have answered the call. To those who still covet the dark let this be known, no mercy will be shown, no quarter will be given. In case you did not understand our reasoning for using David and Celestial as prime examples in this writing, it is because *they can take the heat* whereas others, who are like them, are not yet prepared to do so.

David... Thank you Kato, I shall look forward to seeing you all this night, for there is still much left undone. Ok God, I'm back.

God... Well David, I see you received a touch of Kato's energy field. As you can see it is not quite the same as interacting with others such as yourself. My own energy field is one you integrated with a long time ago, so you more easily adapt to My presence. Your meeting with Kato was a gratifying experience for you. Now that you are semi-back, with at least one foot planted on your beloved planet Earth, let us proceed shall we? Since not everyone will be **personally** interacting with the Masters, I want to touch on a few things you as individuals can do to assist the Masters in helping Terra to continue to usher in the Golden Now. I have spoken to all of you in the past about My NESARA wave. Use it, call it to you in times of need, or when you wish to contribute to the Creative process by thinking aspiring thoughts. Think of the Divine changes you would like to see enter into manifestation here on this world. NESARA is not only conscious; she is capable of intertwining with your thoughts and clearing the way for them, so that their progress is not impeded. She cleanses, purifies, revitalizes and reenergizes and *she displaces,* so choose your thoughts carefully. Call upon her when you feel emotionally or physically tired or drained, she will readily come to your aid as will any of the bevy of Masters, Star Keepers and Spirit Guides who are here on your behalf. Each of you has an entire contingent of Beings at your disposal, remember? Use them well; call upon them to work with you. If you are having trouble formulating a plan of action, or of even maintaining the motivation to keep on going, then ask them for help, this is in great part what they do.

Let me define to you some areas of importance that you may wish to direct your focus on. Education, this is key to invoking any positive changes on a personal or planetary level. The minds and beliefs of the people need to be pointed in the right direction. This is something that each of you can be active participants in. Give *those that ask you,* options for their normal way of relating to life circumstances. When you are not busy performing this function focus your thoughts on healing this planet. The more you send positive reinforcement energy in this pursuit; the sooner Terra's physical vehicle can be restored. Every concentrated effort matters. Now I do not need to tell you which areas are most in need of your help, this should be obvious to everyone. Unfortunately, most humans tend to remain detached from life's dramatic moments until such time as a major catastrophe occurs. **You all need to start doing preventative work**. This is one of the Master's areas of expertise, implementing preventative maintenance measures and counteracting any premeditative actions or events before they occur. Thought is energy, energy is matter and the Masters are "matter" Masters. Remember what Kato said above, he by himself has moved mountains. Imagine what you could accomplish when more than one mind is focused on a single intent. Given that the elements of this world are matter and in a very real sense this entire world is a hologram (with substance), by studying and understanding this fundamental concept you will begin to see how easily some things can be changed by simply reorganizing them. The energy molecules that constitute the makeup of any object, also transforms it to one degree or another. Blue Star the Pleiadian recently spoke in detail of the makeup of energy that flows through the leaves of a tree. He said that if you studied the makeup of the leaves long enough, you can watch them change in front of your eyes. Practice this technique; it can be used on any living matter. While we are on the subject of "matter in dire need of change," I might suggest you focus your intents on the levels of oxygen in the waterways of this world. Water can be revitalized and reenergized by *charging* it. You can assist in this process by focusing your thoughts on this issue and ask the Masters to assist you in this endeavor. If they can move mountains, shift the axis of a planet, or help a race of beings understand how their perceptions are misdirected, I am absolutely sure they can assist you in any endeavor you deem to be of importance.

The Masters will be here as long as their presence is warranted. The more often that people begin the process of calling them in *for all the right reasons,* the greater the numbers of the Masters will increase, until an astounding number of Masters will arrive here to further address the needs of this world. I will now give you an example of what not to do when calling in any evolved Being. Not so long ago a woman, who I will not mention her name, was greatly distressed by the situation her daughter was in with the person she lived with. This woman, who knew better, took it upon herself to call in those magnificent Souls known as **The Thunder Beings,** please note, this is something that should only be done during extreme emergencies. Yet she asked them to do something for her that is considered by Universal Law to be unconscionable. She asked them to murder her daughter's boyfriend. Not only was this wrong, she unintentionally set up a chain of karmic reactions which to this day are still impacting upon her. I will not go into details about these; I will however caution you to always observe the Universal Laws governing Non-Interference before taking any action. There are many things you have within your power to change; interfering in another Soul's personal choices is not one of them. One of the things any good teacher will first teach you is what lines cannot be crossed. Being forewarned is being forearmed. As parts of your material world continue to deteriorate, keep in mind that there are things you can change and others that you are not there to change.

The Masters and I wish to convey to you these following thoughts: When in doubt, seek guidance. When in the know, proceed as if there were no tomorrow. When feeling alone and overwhelmed, call on Us, We will always be by your side. When you feel as if you have done enough, the odds are that you have. When times get tough remember, this IS what you have trained for.

David... God, do you want me to go through all the questions people emailed us and wanted us to ask You after the first "*And Then God Said...*" book came out? I know that this is to be the last "question and answer" format in your "God Book Series." I could pull some of the better ones if you like.

God... No, thank you.

David... And?

God... David, I would prefer if they asked Me themselves. They are going to have to learn to do so eventually, so they may as well get comfortable *dealing* with Me directly. You two have enough placed upon your shoulders with everything that I alone have asked of you.

Children, let others of My Children know that their time for being codependent upon others is up. If they want to know the truth then it is high time they learn for themselves to get the information direct from the horse's mouth. And yes, **I AM still THE Lead Mare.** So all questions from this point on should be *forwarded* here. Don't worry; I do not bite, not often that is. There is no question you should feel unable to ask Me directly. After all, I DO know you better than you know your own Self. David, I think this is as good a place as any to finish this segment of *God Talk*.

God Talk

The Many Faces of Spirituality

Received by Chako Priest, Ph.D.

Chako – Everyone, as he/she changes and transforms, can integrate his or her profession into God's spirituality. That is what life is all about-from the physical to the spiritual-the broadening of the perspective of talking with God that is open to all of us.

God the Father – How is My dear daughter today?

Chako – Much better, thank you (recovering from bronchitis).

God (received by Chako) – Now, Celestial and David have asked for a very interesting topic, for it does lead humanity into higher vibrations. You have asked, "how do people, when they are involved in their purpose in life, their jobs, make that transformation from their jobs to the spiritual aspect?" Some people think that that cannot be so. If you are a person who is in charge of the bowling alley, how can you accommodate that and turn it into something spiritual?

You see how people have a misperception of what Spirituality is. They think it is some type of dogma that you must practice, and that is not correct. Spirituality is a part of you. It is an integration of you. It is your blessed virtues. It is Love; it is Light; it is Acceptance; it is Forgiveness. It is all the goodness that you see in people. So as the person in the bowling alley hands out bowling balls to his customers, all he needs to do is be in his heart and give out the equipment with smiles and good cheer. That My dear friends, is Spirituality.

Since you cannot see any religious overtones in it, you think of it as not being true Spirituality. But that is what I am saying. You see, your religions are man-made, as you have been told. Some refuse to embrace that idea, but that is exactly what is happening. Religions have been so man-made that they have lost their own essence. As Yeshua has said to this Channel, Christianity is not what He remembers it to be. It has become so distorted. So many sects have put their own spin on different verses, His different sayings, His different ideas, that He does not even recognize what they are talking about.

People always seem to tend to make things more complicated than they need to be. Spirituality is simple for it is merely to love, love unconditionally. Love that person who cannot remember his or her way. There has been much ado about nothing, shall we say.

A dear man asked this Channel for her wisdom on what to do when his dear ones are so attuned to their religion that they will not allow any new ideas to change it. She told him that the religions were man-made. And she told him to let it be, to let God. Now I think that is the best advice people can give. Let it go; let it be; let God/ Me into your hearts.

People have misconceived ideas about God the Father. They put Me into these different categories. Some think of Me as a vengeful God. I say that that is not true. Some think of Me as bringing death to them. I say that is not true. Some think of Me as being so high above them that they can never reach Me, and I say that is not true, for you see, I am in your heart. All you need to do, like this Channel did, was to sit down and ask to speak to Me. Since she is so joined with My dear son, Yeshua, He came first. He always comes to her. There is a part of her, you see, that believes that He must come and bring the Beings to her. *(This refers to the Ascended Beings that come forth to give messages through the Channel for the books she transcribes.)* That will change one of these days, for that truly is not correct thinking. She could bring any Being she wishes to her. All of you can, dear Readers; all of you can bring Me, the Father, to you. I am already there. All I would be doing is expressing My thoughts which you would write down or hear in your mind.

We speak *telepathically*, in telepathic terms, as you may call it. But everyone is capable of hearing Me.

Long ago in the era of the dark days, We shall say, when your Master Jesus walked the Earth 2000+years ago, when your Saints and Prophets walked the Earth, people thought that they were not their equals. They could be the shoemaker or the tent-maker and not realize that they too were One with All. They too were One with Me.

Your tent-maker Saint Paul had a fervor, a drive to seek Me and to bring Jesus' Word to the world. He *(Paul)* did not realize that I was with him every step of the way. He did not realize that what he was doing was Spirituality. Any task can be spiritual as long as you are in your heart and you are thinking beautiful thoughts.

It does not always have to be thoughts about Me. That would be a little bit too much, don't you think? But I do love it so when My children consider Me as part of their life, when they wake up in the morning and say, *Good morning Mother/Father God*. And when they go to sleep at night they say, *Thank you, Mother/Father God, for my abundance this day*. That is all they have to do. It is not religious in any way. It is merely recognition that I exist and that I exist in their life. And just maybe My gifts to them rain down and that is why they have abundance.

Everything that they do, you see, with that attitude... their Father's House has no limit. That is Spirituality. People make Spirituality so complicated, as I have said. Events are coming to your world that have been put into action eons ago. These events *are*/were to help Mother Earth so that she would be able to raise her vibrations and make her Ascension. It was known eons ago that people would be ascending during this time.

That is why, My dear friends, it is important for you to make a decision. Are you going more towards Me-more towards Spirituality? Or are you still undecided? It used to be that around the age of 50 was when wisdom would enter people's psyche, shall We say. But the world has sped up so with the introduction of your Internet and your computers that that wisdom level now is really around the age of 40-45. People are wise now. You have a term called *street-wise*. Those people who are street-wise way beyond their years have only to touch the God part, the Me part in their heart and that wise part of themselves that knows humanity could turn into spiritual aspects. That is why your 12-step programs are successful-because those with addictions are from every aspect of life. By joining those 12-step programs, it gets them in touch with their spiritual self.

Now who carries the spiritual self besides Me? It is your soul. Your body is an entity, a wonderful entity, but it is a body-soul, whereas your spiritual self, your Divine self, is your spiritual soul that comes and goes into bodies. It is that part of you that carries your wisdom. If your body is open enough to receive its own soul, then your wisdom will come to you much earlier than anticipated.

Many souls that are coming into bodies these days are coming as walk-ins, and I am sure you have heard about them. They walk into another body that has been prepared, been developed, for it is time consuming to go through all of the child's developmental stages, to come to the point where you are dealing with your karma. Let the soul come forth-let the walk-in soul come, quickly finish up that karma and then get on with its tasks. Each soul carries My signature. Everything you do has a signature of you imprinted within it. It is done with Light-your Light signature. So every deed and misdeed has your signature on it.

People, many people are in so much fear. They fear the unknown. They may be timid souls and they are afraid to go forth and touch unknown circumstances, volunteer for unknown adventures. There are many of you who are millions of years old. You have seen almost everything and have done almost everything positive and negative because you wanted to experience all that is in My Universes. And yet you have only made one wee little step in what is available for you-all the different planets, all the different star systems, all the different Universes, all the different species, all the different people who look like you and may not look like you. They are all there for you to know, for you to mingle with and to love. Some of the species do not know about love. Some of the species only control and you go there to learn these different aspects.

I am known as the God of your heart. I am also known as the God of your Universe. There are places for you to see and touch and feel.

Spirituality-I hope you are getting a picture that encompasses every worldly deed if it comes from love. True Spirituality has its base as love. That is all it is-love. As you know, there are many types of love, but I am talking about the pure love that I send out, the Mother sends out-the love where We are all One. I created you. You are One with Me. It is mankind that raises different people up on pedestals. It is mankind that creates the different strata, the different sects, and the different hierarchies in people.

Why would royalty be better than the man walking the street holding a cup for money to buy food? What makes that difference, for the man with the cup could be the enlightened Master and the man of royalty is still learning his lessons to enlightenment. Royalty goes to church. The man with the cup sits on a park bench and watches the squirrels play among the trees. Which man is truly spiritual? Which man knows Me more? I will let you ponder on this. The answer is very simple. It is the man who asks for little and loves much. It is the man who teaches others how to receive. No one as they pass by knows that person's heart.

Spirituality, dear friends, My dear children, is the simplest concept that you could think of. If you did nothing but be in joy, love Nature, smile to your fellow human beings, love them, do not judge them, bless and forgive the people who turn against you, you would be in Spirituality. You would be closer to God, closer to Me, closer to the Mother, than anyone in church.

I have come this day to tell you that your life is a gift. It is a gift to you, not to be wasted on your addictions. Whether your addiction is to alcohol or food or sex or TV or the Internet, life is not to be an addiction. It is to be loved and lived and enjoyed. It is to realize that you will have the ebb and the flow of good tidings. It is to realize that your body may be ill at times and to honor your body and to know that it will heal when it has run its course. Living a life is a gift from Me.

We have contracts. Many people do not realize this. You stated before you were born what it was you wanted to do with your life. Then, when the veils of forgetfulness came, you found that the life that you had chosen-I had nothing to do with it-you chose that life even to the point where you felt it was not a very productive life. It was not all wine and roses. As some people say, *life sucks*! But that is your choosing; that is not Mine, dear children. I let you use whatever is at your fingertips. Your free will gives you your life. You can turn it to the betterment of your life, or you can turn it to where it is a very dismal prospect.

But it is still your life that you created even before you were born. You created that life. I had nothing to do with it. I give you My love. I watch over you. I know what you are doing but I cannot interfere either. It is your free will. I do not ever interfere.

Therefore, My dear children, this chapter on Spirituality is full of different topics. Each one has Spirituality in it. Are you beginning to see that Spirituality has a broad spectrum? What you do with it is up to you. Of course I want you to come Home. Of course I hold My arms out to you. I am a Parent and I know you have your lessons to learn on the way. I am a Parent waiting for your return and I will receive you with My arms wide open and My love never stopping, for it is a constant flow to you-a constant flow, dear friends, dear children.

May your life be full of joy. May your heart be full of love, for We are One.

I AM God the Father. I have completed this chapter.

Chako – thank you, Father, thank you.

God – you are welcome, My dear child. This will be an unusual chapter, so we will see what Celest and David wish to do with it. My blessings to you, dear one.

(Chako Priest is a Transpersonal Psychologist, Author, and Telepathic Channel. You can read more about her and her books at our website www.godumentary.com

Our Response

We appreciate the fact that our beloved friend Chako took the time to spend with God to write this chapter for this book. It is always a delightful time for us when we read what another "vessel" has written about their conversations with a highly evolved Source. We believe that God expressed Himself very well; He as usual, made many salient points about the truth of Spirituality and the core problems with religions. God, we applaud you for speaking on the topic of Spirituality and the "common man." And also touching on the situations that people usually do not want to hear about. Oddly enough, people become nervous and feel unsettled when coping with a homeless person or a street peddler. We wonder how many people ever stop to consider that the person they are "in avoidance of," could be Jesus The Christ wearing a human form. Of course we are in agreement that Jesus' words have become bastardized. It is what people do. If they can not understand the words or if they pore over the meanings and still do not understand, they then change the words to suit what THEY think the words should be. No one on the planet should ever "edit" Jesus' words or God's words. That could make the ride to Nirvana a very long walk for them instead!

Celest and David

From the Continuum

God *(received by Celest)* Well, Children, if you were expecting Me to write this book for the purpose of indulging in witty banter and darling dainty anecdotes, then no doubt you are now very disappointed. Be aware that I have not set aside the time to write these books simply because I have too much "time" on My hands. My books are intended to be a mass communication that is to be used as a means to an end. I am not writing these books to justify all that We must continue to do here, but rather to be able to keep you, *the Children,* in harmony with yourself as individual Souls and as pioneers of the collective consciousness. Many, many, years ago I also tried to do this in order to avert the mass dissolution of humanity. Had that event taken place, it would have eventually caused ALL of the Earthbound races here to simply exterminate themselves. We managed to avert that crisis back then, because of the numerous goodhearted Souls on this planet who worked so hard with Me as We tried to alleviate "the human condition." We did so by counterbalancing that situation with love and as much Light as was available through the hearts of people AT THAT TIME. If We had not been able to alter that precarious situation then, here is what would have happened. This world would now be in anarchy. It would have been the likes of which NONE of you have ever seen before. Obviously, I am not referring to anything political! My intent along with the desires of the Creator, was to attempt to teach *you Children of the human races,* of the pure necessity of aligning yourselves, of "pledging your allegiance" to that of the Creation processing. To do less than this would be to ultimately seal your own personal and planetary destinies in a manner that none of you could possibly survive.

Ergo, out of necessity We had to rethink the Earth situation while maintaining a watchful eye on the planetary repercussions that would have without a doubt taken place, as piecemeal assaults rendered worthless and useless the plight of the human races to reclaim themselves. Nor would they have been able to assist in the Creation of a finer world here. This is how in one fell swoop it was decided that a dedicated communiqué between MySelf and all the Earthbound Children would be the most advantageous manner to *"reach out and touch someone."* In this case, MANY someones. This Children, is the reason beyond the reason of why I have been chosen to write these books. I speak with you each from the continuum, yet in a larger than life sense, **I AM the continuum.** Although I have been doing My best to write as simply as possible, some things are just too complex for the average individual to truly understand. When this occurs I search for certain words in all of your languages that correctly correspond with the meanings I am trying to share with you all.

A truly not unexpected oddity occurred though while writing the previous two books. Although it saddens Me to have to tell you this, many well-intentioned people who read the first two books, people who were in most cases ecstatic to hear My words of truth, simply forgot some of My more pivotal points. You see, when people are reading My words, I have My own rather unique way of monitoring their emotions, gauging their "reality checks," and observing their levels of Spiritual maturity either rising or lowering in accordance to their understanding of My written words. Although all of Us who are the Luminescents have the ability to do this, in My own case it was to see, hear, feel and touch those who were learning, those who were not and those who were reading these books simply seeking some type of self-gratification. Some of the points of Light that I had been so intent on sharing with all people in order to further their understanding and thereby negating the useless and self-effacing illusions they had been believing, fell by the wayside due to "*lack of use.*" In other words if you do not use it...you lose it... and that is what happened to many readers.

So from My vantage point, I saw that I had but one option left, I have had to intentionally repeat certain information. I have stated the information in slightly different ways as a means to try **one last time** to impress upon all what I perceive as the great need for the understanding that each reader should have. This is to ensure that the good Souls reading these books have the information to learn from and to be better able to survive the present and the coming times. Do not be concerned about what may happen if a person who does not qualify as "a good person," decides to read any of the God book Series. First of all, they would be contemptuous of even the thought of reading these books. Secondly, if perchance some of them did so out of sheer curiosity, perhaps they would decide to leave their erstwhile beliefs and would actually learn something about the greater truths! I can hope anyway.

OK, now that I have released a bit of God steam, I have decided that if people do not bother to pay attention to the messages I am giving, then in the last five of these books, I will not make any effort to repeat information that has already been stated, unless there is some type of "just cause" to do so. I am hoping there will not be!

Children, over the last six months I have watched so many of you swinging to and fro between belief and disbelief, as you watch and listen to what other people on this planet are doing and saying. Your hearts have been swinging like pendulums, and yet as you looked more deeply and had more candid thoughts regarding the ongoing situations here, it is with great heartfelt relief that I can now say to you, because you are undergoing this non-analytical process, you are making tremendous strides. *You are succeeding in altering your beliefs without remorse, without seeking redress, without feeling a need to defend your beliefs.* You have finally learned that defending truth actually invalidates it. **Truth must always stand on its own!** You have each as separate entities always been resilient. But now, Children, now you shine so much greater and so much more easily than you ever have before...in this lifetime that is. Your resiliency knows no bounds. This is but one reason why the collective consciousness is reaching out to you and for you, like a full complement of matchsticks in a new book of matches. If I seem to speak harshly at times, it is only because of an ongoing situation I am trying to curb. Here is the situation: although many of you hear the truth of My words, you understand the intensity and depth and levels of My writings, you still are unable to see or hear beyond what YOU KNOW. Therefore, I feel that it is important for you to learn to feel beyond what I say, hear beyond what I tell you and sense beyond the obvious. In this manner none can cause your Souls to feel emaciated, none can cause your beliefs to be emasculated and none can cause you to feel worthless, or dronish. Nor are you clones. I am filled with joyous fatherly pride as I gaze upon your upturned Souls; each Soul striving ever more diligently as It seeks a state of perfection of ItSelf. Although that state can only be achieved here in the continuum, it is the ever striving energy that alters the Soul status, and that is as it should be!

Children, learn what you can, while you can. Never be concerned that you will in any way let Me down. That is not how I see Souls. A Soul may experience disappointment with ItSelf, however I do not. OK, Children, understand Me clearly now, please: the simple fact that I am able to see what you do not, should confirm to you each that when I tell you that *you are really succeeding,* then you should KNOW that it is true. I am telling you that now. Here in the continuum all things are made manifest indeed. Nothing can be hidden, no secrets kept. Please Children, bear in mind what I have tried to tell you so many times before: "Life is a continuous journey of self-exploration, enjoy yours." I know I do!

The Greatest Challenge of All

Although as scribes we are always able to adapt very quickly to writing whatever material God dictates to us, He has said He does not want us to read any of the God book series until the last of the eight books are written. So when people speak with us about the books that are already in print and ask us questions about something that God has said, we usually draw a blank. We do not talk about what God has said because we do not know what He said anyway! It is a very unusual situation at times; we simply have no memory of what we had written and because God does not want us to read the books yet, we can not say what we do not know. That is the practical explanation!

On a completely different level of understanding, we know that God is adamant about people formulating their own decisions regarding things He has said. We know many people who invariably find that it is always easier to ask another's opinion than it is to actually work out the answers for themselves. Why? Life is not the easiest "conveyance to heaven" as it is, so why make things more complicated than they need to be? Yes, we know that people have the ability to stimulate their minds through the questioning process, but inevitably they find that if they try too hard or for too long to arrive at reasonable analogies for something they have read, they only become more confused. *Sometimes the written word is just that,,, nothing more and nothing less.* In other words, if you try to put everything in life under an intellectual microscope, whether it is about what God is saying or about what your intellect is telling you, you stand a better than even chance of forgetting *or losing* the information that is truly at the heart of the matter.

That having been said we want to address an issue that is of great importance to you. No, we have not discussed this with God, this is Celest and David, with our own combined thoughts of what is of primary importance to you each, individually and collectively. Because everyone here is either standing on a precipice, falling into it or leaping over it, all that you each do everyday from here on in, will prove to be the greatest challenge you each must confront. You do not have to be a rocket scientist to know that people on the planet are unhappy with themselves and unhappy with others as well. The great "depression" is now, "*the great discontent.*" Personally we are relived that it is! Although that is a sad statement, we feel it aptly describes what had been so needed here on the Earth Star planet in order for people living under the Universal Law of cause and effect, to cease their mindless pursuits in life and concentrate on having a real life.

It is most unfortunate that so many good people here are losing so much. It is also a very sad situation to see how few of them truly understand why this has come to be and how so many of them knowingly or unknowingly, have contributed to this "*state of the union.*" People who are stuck in "Semantics 101" should have a field-day with that last statement of ours. People who needed to grow up and accept personal responsibility for their own ill-conceived contribution to the mess Earth is in, are now having to confront themselves, BY themselves.

Yes, that horrible term, "collateral damage" comes to mind as we watch other people, those who truly exemplify goodness and Light struggling to hold on to their very sanity. Although the majority of those experiencing the deepest distress are unaware of this, they are slowly being gathered together by an invincible Universal bond and becoming a part of the collective consciousness. This pleases us greatly! "Alone," people can only withstand so much despair and anxiety without becoming worn and exhausted beyond belief. That is the danger zone! That is when a person has the greatest susceptibility for giving up. We do know from what God has spoken to us about in the past, and the innate knowledge that we brought with us to this planet, that this is but one reason why the collective consciousness is so greatly needed now. "Alone together," is a mutual sharing; it is *the call for all good Souls to unite now."*

This collective is far more than mutual sharing of beliefs; it is about caring unconditionally for others without any bias or bigotry. It is a co-joining of Creative endeavors to teach the hungry how to feed themselves when no one else can. It is understanding the natural alternatives to use to Create a better, healthier life. It is the quiet and seldom spoken of understanding that as each one in the collective shares their wealth, whether it is monetary or Spiritual, with those who have less, or nothing at all, that they are further spreading the Jesus The Christ consciousness like a massive wave over, around, below and above this planet. Everyone has some final decisions to make here and now. Are you or CAN you lose vanity, arrogance or false pride and recant any illusionary or delusionary beliefs? Are you able to **STAND** as a proactive cluster of true human beings bent on the reformation of this planet rather than on the destruction of Earth? All must do so *without any expectations of receiving less than they should.* Yes, this may be a massive trust issue for many. Is it better to try and fail or not to try at all? You each must decide that for yourselves.

Ultimately, whatever choice each person makes will be the deciding factor in this, the greatest challenge of all.

Remember, you can stand ALONE or you can STAND alone TOGETHER.

Celest and David

Our Biographies

Celestial Blue Star and David of Arcturus
We're still Standing

God
I Am Too

Books currently available
from Celest and David

And Then God Said... Then I Said... Then He Said...
Volume One - first book of the God Book series.

Beyond the Veil ~ Epiphanies from God
Gods Truths and Revelations for Today and Tomorrow
Book number 2 of the God Book Series

And Then God Said... Then I Said... Then He Said...
Volume Two - third book of the God Book series.

Blue Star the Pleiadian
My Teachings through Transmissions
A Three Volume Series

Star Tek - **Perspectives through Technology**
Volume One

Star Tek Volume 2 by Celest, David and Ningishzida will be written in-between the writings of our other books. Send us your suggestions and alternative energy ideas for possible inclusion for us to write about in the next volume.

Send an e-mail to admin@awakenedhearts.com

Celest and David's Websites

www.bluestarspeaks.com

www.awakenedhearts.com

www.godumentary.com

New Book News-On July-11-2010 Celest was told that God wanted us to write a complete series of His books. David later talked to God about this matter and was told that this was predestined long, long, ago. God has said that there will be a total of eight books in the God Book series. In accordance with this new responsibility we will post the titles of these upcoming books. Stay tuned for these and more from Celest and David...

The entire God Book series consists of:

#1 And Then God Said... Then I Said... Then He Said... Volume One

#2 Beyond the Veil~Epiphanies from God

#3 And Then God Said... Then I Said... Then He Said... Volume Two

#4 The Code

#5 Beyond the Journey

#6 Advocates for Justice

#7 Winter People who Ride the Wind

#8 Avatars in the Valley of the Ancients

http://rainbowproducts.awakenedhearts.com/